MW00611524

EVERYDAYNESS

Intentional Practices for
Seeing, Being & Doing
in a Post-Pandemic World

Foreword by Robby Kenner,
Oscar-Nominated & Emmy Winning Filmmaker of *Food, Inc.*

Mike Morrison, Ph.D.

Publishing services provided by Archangel Ink | archangelink.com

 www.linkedin.com/in/mike-morrison-ph-d-580b0b14

Paperback ISBN: 978-1-950043-53-8
Hardback ISBN: 978-1-950043-54-5

Praise for *Everydayness*

"Most of us don't take the time to contemplate how meaningful our lives are. We're too busy. Everydayness *inspires a blueprint for moment-by-moment gratitude, for conscious quality of every waking hour. If we all agree that life is terribly short, this book gives some relief to that pressure. It offers a path to conscious meaning and joy on a daily basis. If you're seeking to define and connect with the values you cherish, consider* Everydayness *your crucial guide."*

– Diana Nyad–At age 64 completed the historic swim from Cuba to Florida, 111 miles in 53 hours. The subject of the Netflix film *NYAD*, starring Annette Bening and Jodie Foster.

"Brilliant work! The post pandemic world has created significant challenges, changes and chaos, leaving us all trying to figure out how to thrive and not just survive. Mike has delivered a practical approach on how to adapt and transform moments into meaning along the "everydayness" journey. Everydayness *addresses the needed focus on well-being and self-care and is an invaluable guide to fulfill one's own life to the greatest extent. My own "brand" of* Everydayness *has started with the tools provided by Mike!"*

– Kimberly Russo, CEO, George Washington University Hospital, Group Vice President DC Region

"Throughout my career, I've spent considerable time thinking about concepts like calling and purpose. Mike simplifies this into a more accessible question; 'What would you be doing every day in your most meaningful life?' In reframing the way we approach this idea and many others, his book has helped me rethink my own rituals and rhythms in new and profound ways. With fresh tools and concepts, Everydayness *has helped me move toward greater levels of presence, meaning, and thoughtfulness in my personal and work life."*

– Jim Howe, Chief Operating & Financial Officer, Door of Hope

"*In his book* Everydayness, *Mike Morrison offers a thoughtful exploration of how to find more meaning in our daily life, reminding us of the power we have to make every moment matter for a sustained sense of well-being and happiness.*"

   – Rebecca Braitling, Co-founder of UpSpiral Leadership

"*In this short but richly layered book, Morrison crystalizes years of research and practice into the concept of Everydayness. He masterfully articulates a model for personal growth rooted in the meaning-making practices of appreciation, purpose, and thoughtful sensemaking. Everydayness is a great model for living a purposeful, intentional, and meaningful life. For leaders it is a pathway to discovering your leadership potential and a powerful model for those who want to make a difference in their small world and a meaningful impact on the people they are privileged to lead and serve.*"

   – Michael Johnson, President, Span Alaska

"*In* Everydayness, *Morrison reveals unexpected lessons and insights from the pandemic while sharing three simple but life-changing practices for how we can live our days in the most purposeful ways. Prepare to change!*"

   – Matthew Orlando, General Counsel, Kenvue

"*With* Everydayness, *Morrison succeeds in laying out a path for living a meaningful and purpose-driven life in the midst of our world of constant distractions and false pursuits. Everydayness is a terrific guide for anyone looking to reclaim their life and live each day more fully.*"

   – Peggy Kennedy, Author, "Approaching Neverland, A Memoir of Epic Tragedy and Happily-Ever-After"

"*One of the delights in Mike Morrison's new book is the way he nests his exploration of "everydayness" in everyday, accessible language. He speaks plainly and directly, as a writer who invites you into his thoughts in a generous, welcoming spirit of companionship. Join him!*"

   – Paul Vandeventer, Founder, Community Partners

"Mike's remarkable ability to simplify complex concepts into clear, transformative insights makes this book a deeply impactful read. He reveals how the essence of life's meaning is often found in the everyday experiences we overlook, encouraging us to pause and appreciate them. His reflections offer both deep introspection and practical approaches to finding wholeness and connecting with the core of our humanity."

– Michael Estrada, CEO, SAG-AFTRA Health Plan and SAG Pension Plan

"What is the highest and best use of your time? Everydayness *can be your companion guide to answering this question. This is a book in which every page offers deep meaning. It made me want to read it slowly . . . and fully discover the wisdom within it.*

– Joel Wright, President, Leadership Forum Community

"Everydayness. Mike makes this concept so amazingly clear and beautiful that you simply cannot ignore its importance."

– Lynne Barnes, Chief People Officer

"A must read for those of us striving for meaningful lives. Morrison shares life-changing insights into how we can rethink the rhythms of how we live our days."

– Bernie Jaworski, Ph.D., Peter F. Drucker Chair in Management and the Liberal Arts, Claremont Graduate University

Foreword

"Making a movie is telling a story that resonates with others. Living a life is creating a story that resounds with our own internal audience. Everydayness helps us shape our story in profound ways."
— Robby Kenner

We all love a good story. They inspire us, offer new perspectives, and prompt self-reflection. In my work as a documentary film-maker, I endeavor to look behind the veil to truly understand how a system works. I am also drawn to the stories that illuminate the profound connections between how we live our lives and the broader world we inhabit. In my film *Food, Inc.* and its sequel, *Food, Inc. 2,* I've sought to reveal the complex narratives behind the food we eat and how multinational corporations control the food system at enormous cost to our environment and our personal well-being.

Morrison's *Everydayness* is an illuminating guide for shaping our personal stories. He artfully peels back the layers of our daily existence and offers a compelling new roadmap loaded with practical advice and illuminating insights from others like us. Here's where it gets interesting. As a filmmaker and human being, it is not lost on me the compelling parallels between making a movie and bringing our own story to life.

Just as our lives are directed by dreams, goals, and aspirations, a movie starts with a script and a director's vision. Both require a clear sense of direction and purpose or our progress will be thwarted. The *Everydayness* chapter "Purpose" reveals a simple but powerful intention-setting practice that can keep our dreams on track.

In life, we face unforeseen obstacles daily and must be flexible, adjusting our well-laid plans on a moment's notice. During production, filmmakers must adapt (continuously!) to unexpected challenges and find creative solutions.

Finally, films often go through multiple edits to achieve the best result. Similarly, life involves continuous learning and self-improvement, refining our actions and choices over time. As humans, we are always in "edit" mode and in the "Sensemaking" chapter, Morrison shares a critical meaning-making process for dealing with the unexpected, confusing, and emotional issues that can disrupt the flow of our day.

Whether you are a teacher, nurse, chef, entrepreneur or a filmmaker like me, *Everydayness* will be your "every day" guide to discovering that meaning is not elusive or just over the horizon – but is discovered in the act of living each day. As Morrison wisely notes: "We don't have to create it. We just need to learn to see it, appreciate it, and fully experience it."

I am honored to lend my voice to this important work, and I believe that it will inspire you to live each day with greater awareness and intention . . . as your unique story unfolds.

Sincerely,
Robby Kenner

Dedication

To all the cats and dogs in my life and yours.
They bring a joy and meaning that goes way beyond their
short lives. I cannot imagine a world without them.

Contents

Preface

Here's my question.

To what degree do our days feel like we are living the "If …
then" life? In other words, *if* this happens … *then* life will be
great.

If … then is the provisional life. It is the life that feels like it is just
over the horizon. It is the life that will complete us. It sounds
like this:

> *If I get that promotion, secure this relationship, clear the decks
> of all this messiness, get my work life in order … actually, get
> my whole life in order … it is then … at last … that I will be in
> control and true meaning can be found. My life can truly begin.*

Sadly, it never happens. Or at least not in the way we envision.

I certainly fell prey to living the provisional life prior to finding
truer sources of meaning.

In the process I learned to accept that there will always be too
much to do and most of it doesn't matter.

I also learned that few important experiences are painless, and there's lots of good news in that realization.

Finally, meaning in life is best found within us and through the moments that make up our days.

Welcome to *everydayness*.

Introduction
Reclaiming Our Days

"'What day is it?'
'It's today,' squeaked Piglet.
'My favorite day,' said Pooh."
— A.A. Milne

Prior to the pandemic, our days could often be dulled by everyday activities that repeated. We ate the same breakfast. Took the same commute to and from work. Beyond these routines were the unplanned distractions and ongoing urgencies that characterized our challenging and stressful work lives. Plus, the logistical nature of a modern life was numbing in nature as we continually shopped for food and other things, arranged car pools for the kids, scheduled ongoing appointments for whatever, and tried to stay ahead of a to-do list that was always growing in size and complexity.

We added to the chaos by surrendering to the ethos of a screen-driven world that can capture much of our waking days as we overconsumed whatever popular culture was feeding us. Not surprisingly, the many new technologies were as limiting as they were liberating. For many, popular and hopelessly addictive social media platforms (like TikTok, Meta, Instagram) offered some temporary relief from the always-on anxiety that followed us through the day. These fragmented patterns that made up our days kept us longing for what really matters.

But here is where it gets interesting.

This all got interrupted when the worldwide pandemic occurred in early 2020. The onset of the virus quickly erased what little sense of control we had in our lives. The world was already moving too fast and in chaotic patterns that often left us humbled. The routines that gave us some sense of coherence were now gone:

> *Dropping the kids off to school on our way to work.*
> *Using the drive in to work to prepare for the day.*
> *Stopping at the gym on the way home from work.*

Almost overnight, these routines disappeared—and so did our sense of order. Plus, everything felt at risk. Our jobs. Our relationships. Our plans for the future.

Despite the potential dire consequences of a global health catastrophe, it was amazing to see how we responded. Our first instinct was to hunker down, but it didn't take long for new routines to emerge. Zoom and other popular "live" conferencing services quickly became the new conduit for business meetings and connecting with family. Even "happy hours" and family holiday gatherings moved to these face-friendly digital platforms.

Amazingly, we also saw meaning-making in the self-sacrifice and caring for others that reached heroic levels among our health care and front-line service workers. They were continually pressed to their limits as they became our "essential" providers in an uncertain world. You would not have thought that a rational calculation of the unknown and the inherent health risks would lead to such levels of self-sacrifice.

But despite our deep survival instincts, we saw many move beyond self-interest and serve. We got to witness what Holocaust survivor Viktor Frankl called our "will to meaning" as humans. It is the natural pull to search for meaning and purpose in our lives, even under the most dire circumstances. Bella, a nurse in New York City, reflected these sentiments in our 2020 interview:

"It was overwhelming to witness death on a daily, sometimes hourly, basis. I was emotionally exhausted. I desperately wanted to quit but knew I would leave my friends shorthanded. So I did my nurse role the best I could. Doing my twelve-hour shifts. Keeping patients comfortable and hopefully improving. And while holding the hand of a patient who was passing ... it hit me. With family members restricted by the quarantine, I realized I was the last person she would experience in her life. I have never felt more present to someone. Forever it changed how I view our patients ... and how I view myself."

If you look closely at this reflection, it is loaded with a newfound sense of purpose and meaning. Amazingly, as people leaned into the necessary sensemaking required by the pandemic, more positive and meaningful framings started to surface. These initial framings further evolved into new identities. It doesn't end there.

Ultimately, these meaning-making reflections would become a part of our larger narrative or life story. How powerful!

From these stories and many others, I saw the potential for a new kind of normal to emerge in our post-pandemic world. After all, I had spent the previous two decades researching, writing books, and trying to untangle the role of meaning in our everyday lives. I discovered along the way how meaning is the only thing that can fully counter the anxiety, isolation, and confusion of a contemporary life. So it was no surprise to find that meaning-making emerged as a natural response to the fears of a pandemic-sized health crisis. Also not surprising is that I soon found myself immersed in what felt like the next chapter in my life's work—this book!

> *"Historically, pandemics have forced humans to break with the past and imagine their world anew. This one is no different. It is a portal, a gateway between one world and the next."*
> — **Arundhati Roy**

With all the extra time the pandemic lockdown afforded, I continued my research with a big heart. I wanted to understand more deeply how meaning could become more integrated into our everyday lives. I wanted to explore how we could facilitate meaning-making without the shock of a trauma-inducing event. Building on two decades of personal research and application work with over thirty different organizations, I reached out to other researchers, practitioners, and just about anyone who would have a conversation on the topic. I did ongoing survey research, collecting data from hundreds of participants. I was all in and ...

... as new insights on meaning evolved, so did I.

My focus was now shifting to the special nature of *meaningful moments* and the promise that much of the meaning we could discover was already present in our lives. That's a pause point: *much of the meaning we can discover is already present in our lives.* We don't have to create it. We just need to learn to see it, appreciate it, and fully experience it. I still remember the day when I landed on the word that captured the essence of living our lives more completely by experiencing the moments of the day more fully:

Everydayness.

It captures the heart of our journey on the following pages and beyond. I believe it has the potential to change your life. It certainly has changed mine.

A special note: While I curated many of the ideas that follow, much credit is due to the thought-provoking and scholarly insights from a range of thought leaders that are highlighted within the book. They bring both support and understanding to the concepts of *everydayness* that I could not do on my own.

The book is equally enriched by the real-world experiences and stories from people I've had the privilege to serve in my work. These voices, which are presented throughout the book, evolved from my deep personal experiences in supporting over thirty organizations during the last fifteen years as a management consultant, author/speaker, and educator.

The ongoing relationships developed mostly through intensive in-person training programs (and are well-represented in my nearly 3,000 followers on LinkedIn). The training themes included leadership development, personal and professional development, lean thinking (from my Toyota experience), and emotional intelligence. The diversity of these organizations is significant and includes:

- Major consumer brands like Lexus, Nike, Harley-Davidson, Johnson & Johnson, and Avery-Dennison.

- Prominent health care systems, including the Ronald Reagan UCLA Medical Center, Providence Saint Joseph Medical Center, and the Keck Hospital of USC.

- Other wonderful partners were tech organizations, including Juniper Networks and Netstock; MAS (a major apparel manufacturer in Sri Lanka); Span Alaska (a leader in the freight industry); education innovators like Chappaqua School District in New York; and PATH, a nonprofit organization providing comprehensive homeless services.

- Dozens of individual coaching relationships (with entrepreneurs, students, teachers, parents, writers, and athletes) add to the diversity.

I am thankful to these participants for their contributions to *everydayness* and my personal growth. I am also grateful for the many connections that have transformed into lasting friendships.

This book is for you if:

You want to create more time and space for the meaningful parts of your work and life *but feel like you are often pulled in meaningless directions with limited progress.*

More than anything you want to feel a strong sense of purpose, that "what you do" and "who you are" truly matters. Let's get after it!

Onward,

Mike Morrison
June, 2024

Chapter One
Everydayness

A simple and purposeful rhythm to life

*"How we spend our days is, of course,
how we spend our lives."*
— Annie Dillard

Key Themes	Questions We Will Answer
Exploring Everydayness	*What is "everydayness" and how does it facilitate meaning in life?*
Meaning Matters Most	*What are the key sources of meaning in our daily lives?*
Everyday Practices	*How do we translate the sources of meaning into everyday practices?*

Exploring Everydayness

As revealed in the introduction, the pandemic opened my eyes as to how *meaning* could be more fully leveraged in the everyday moments that make up the natural flow of life. When the pandemic took away many of the routines that gave a sense of meaning to our lives, we were left to rediscover where to re-find that meaning. In our quarantined, isolated existence, I became fascinated with how seemingly "small" experiences (e.g., savoring a cup of coffee, a walk in the neighborhood, a phone chat with a friend) became increasingly significant sources of that lost meaning.

Over the last twenty years, the subject of meaning has been central to my work. In short, it is what I think about most. It started with a leadership book I authored (*Leading Through Meaning*) when I was the founder and dean of the University of Toyota. Since then I've authored other books (including *The Other Side of the Card* and *Creating Meaningful Change*) while engaging in ongoing research. I've also integrated the principles of meaning deeply into my current leadership and organizational development practice. But it was the new revelations from the pandemic that excited me most. I became immersed in focusing all of this previous knowledge and experience into bringing meaning more fully into our daily lives in a life-enhancing practice I call:

Everydayness

Let's start by taking a closer look at the word. By adding "ness" to "everyday," it communicates the "quality of being every day." It connotes a powerful state of being. We live our lives in days, and what we do daily has the best chance of becoming part of *who we are and what we can become.* No one said it better than Annie Dillard:

"How we spend our days, of course, is how we spend our lives."

It follows then: How should we live our days? That is the question I hope to answer deeply through *everydayness.* In essence, it is the daily practice of leading oneself in a world where we must increasingly accept that we alone play the dominant role in shaping our lives. As humans, we yearn to make sense of the world, transcend our limitations, and align to our unique calling in life. Unfortunately, life can feel like a string of disconnected events. Through *everydayness*, we gain empowering perspectives that make us whole and protect us from the fragmentation and meaningless logistics of a modern life.

The principles and practices that bring *everydayness* to life have fully emerged over the last five years and have been supported and refined through dozens of real-world application opportunities. We begin with a definition of *everydayness*:

> *A meaning-centered and daily-driven*
> *pathway for living our lives.*

That's it. It's simple, but through *everydayness* we learn how meaning is the essential psychological resource that repurposes daily events, both positive and negative, in a way that strengthens us.

To do so requires that we acknowledge that a life comes with both highs and lows, joy and sadness, wins and losses. If we can learn to experience our emotions in new ways, we can be enriched by these polar opposites. Together we will deeply discover how these sources of meaning can become the natural rhythms, routines, and rituals of the day.

These meaning-centered practices are needed now more than ever as we learn to work in our hybrid work cultures. We now struggle as homebound free agents trying to make progress and collaborate in an increasingly mentor-less, less-connected, less-relational work world. But these practices are a necessary response to our American culture (and others for sure) that tends to be overly-centered on achievement, success, and how we compare to others. As a result, we can get stuck in the failures and regrets of the past or become preoccupied with our dreams for a better future. In our exploration, we will come to grips with the stark reality that ...

> *Living too much in the past or future comes at*
> *the expense of finding meaning today.*

In other words, carrying the burdens of the past or overinvesting in an uncertain future makes it difficult to find meaning in our present-moment life. Paradoxically, the reverse is even more true.

> *How we experience and find meaning in the present*
> *moments of today determines our future.*

That's a keeper! Our exploration in this book will be a success if together we can fully grasp that statement, which gets to the heart of *everydayness*. While the past will always follow us in some way (for good or bad), our *everydayness* approach will bring more focus to the moments and opportunities that make up each day. Unfortunately, most moments are fleeting and barely recognized in our consciousness. This is often due to a mindless busyness that can easily capture a day. We get fooled into thinking that all the activity and spontaneous reactions are moving us forward. While the busyness may make us feel important (*I must be important ... look how busy I am*) and protect us from experiencing our own existential angst (*who am I, really?*), it never leads to any deeper meaning.

Meaning Matters Most

As revealed in the introduction, the pandemic reaffirmed my belief that the pursuit of meaning is what defines us most as human beings. Neither celebrity nor success nor happiness can rival the life-giving power of meaning. Here's the cool thing— experiencing meaning in life serves as the ultimate protector against anxiety, depression, and other life limitations.[1] Unfortunately, the complexity, confusion, and busyness that overly defines our contemporary lives can dramatically interfere with the one thing that can bring wholeness to our fragmented lives:

Meaning.

John Gardner's timeless definition of meaning gets to the heart of it. The paragraph below captures the true spirit of meaning, *something we build into our life.*[2] It is a framing that has inspired me for much of my life and still resonates with me today. It's worth reading a couple of times to let it truly sink in. Gardner was Secretary of Health, Education, and Welfare under President Lyndon Johnson and is best known for his inspiring writings, where meaning was always a central theme. He once received a letter from a father in Colorado who recently lost his twenty-year-old daughter in an auto accident. He noted to Gardner that his quote below was found in her wallet, and it pleased him to know such sentiments were held near to her heart.

"Meaning is not something you stumble across, like the answer to a riddle or the prize in a treasure hunt. Meaning is something

you build into your life. You build it out of your own past, out of your affections and loyalties, out of the experience of humankind as it is passed on to you, out of your own talent and understanding, out of the things you believe in, out of the things and people you love, out of the values for which you are willing to sacrifice something. The ingredients are there. You are the only one who can put them together into that unique pattern that will be your life. Let it be a life that has dignity and meaning for you."

In other words, it is not just achieving milestones or overcoming significant challenges that produce meaning. Meaning can be *built into* our days, an energizing and sustaining force that builds … moment by moment.

One of my favorite prescriptions for finding meaning in our days is Garrison Keillor's sign-off from his radio show on Minnesota Public Radio. He would end his show with the following:

"Be well, do good work, and keep in touch."

It is great advice, a simple but wonderful formula for both a meaningful day and a meaningful life. I especially love the expression: *do good work.* I interpret it as … *it's not about me being great, but doing work that has a goodness to it … serving others.*

Author and Holocaust survivor Viktor Frankl (*Man's Search for Meaning*) would certainly second that emotion. Meaning brought him through the suffering of the Holocaust and formed the basis for his entire approach to life and his work as a therapist. How can we go about finding meaning? Frankl offers some of the best advice: "One should *not* search for an abstract meaning of life."[3] In other words, Frankl believes that meaning should not be pursued as a goal in itself. It must ensue as a side-benefit of pursuing goals and aspirations that connect you with something beyond yourself. That is not always easy to do in a world that can put a spotlight on happiness rather than meaning.

Like our search for meaning, the pursuit of happiness is also one of our central motivations in life.[4] Most of us probably don't believe we need a formal definition of happiness. We know it when we feel it, and we often use the term to describe a range of positive emotions, including joy, contentment, and gratitude. Most people strongly equate happiness with the "good life," things like a rich family life, great relationships, secure and satisfying work, freedom to pursue interests, and opportunities to travel. You get the idea.

Interestingly, when I ask *"What experiences have brought great meaning to your life?"* the responses start to shift toward how they prevailed over significant challenges or the lessons learned in a major setback. The simple use of the word *meaning* triggers this swing. The whole tone starts to change as the participants recount compelling stories or moments of truth that produced great meaning in their lives. Some of the stories started as follows:

> *We were about to lose everything we worked for ...*
> *Against my advice, she stood up to the bully ...*
> *It was a moment of truth in our relationship ...*

Still, the things that tend to get the most attention in our achievement- and consumption-focused cultures are things like money, status, job promotions, beautiful homes, and great vacations, even though we know that the relationship between these things and happiness is elusive. For example:

> *We desperately seek a promotion at work, one that we believe will bring us happiness in its prestige and enhanced compensation. Somehow we are convinced that this new job will change just about everything in our life for the positive. Soon after receiving the promotion, the increased responsibility, pressures, and hours actually detract from our life satisfaction. The anticipated new levels of happiness never materialize. We may even start to wonder if the trade-offs are worth it.*

As Frankl discovered, it is our capacity to shape meaning in service to something larger than ourselves that makes life worth living.[5] We have all experienced those transformational moments when we are called into service in some special way. It might be a family member that needs help facing a crisis. Or a major work challenge that calls upon our special skills. It is often in these unique situations that meaning comes to life most. It is situations like these that can help us to realize that …

We are at our best when we are needed.

Inspired by Gardner, Keillor, Frankl, and many, many more, I will try to bring the same "grounding" to the meaning we seek in our everyday lives. One of my key strategies will be to focus on the "little" meanings that naturally make up our day.

It could be that first sip of coffee in the morning, a special connection with a colleague at work, significant progress on a key goal, or a breakthrough idea that comes in the shower at the end of the day. We will see how a "meaningful moment" can be transforming.

We will also explore what psychologists and researchers would identify as the key sources of meaning in life and leverage them in the *everydayness* strategies that follow.[6] I refer to them as the three "sense-abilities." When these feelings are present, life feels meaningful, we begin to thrive, and a sense of well-being emerges.

> **Sense of Appreciation**: I can fully experience the moments of life itself—and thus fully experience and appreciate the true meaning in things.

> **Sense of Purpose**: My life is motivated and directed by valued goals, and this positive focus creates meaning for me.

> **Sensemaking**: My life experiences make sense to me, and this helps me to attach and receive meaning from them.

Let's get a real feel for these three sources with the experience of two new college students:

Case One: Stephen is guided by his high school counselor and family members toward accounting because of his strength in math and the ready-made options of an accounting career. Let's review the three sources after the first year of studies:

Sense of Appreciation: The experience itself of studying accounting is less than satisfying and often feels stressful and de-energizing for Stephen.

Sense of Purpose: Stephen certainly derives some meaning from being in college and on the way toward a solid career.

Sensemaking: While Stephen enjoys math, his experience with accounting principles is not the same. He struggles to make sense out of accounting logic, and his grades are reflecting it.

Case Two: Angela has always been interested in what makes "people tick" and took an introductory psychology course at the local community college as a senior in high school. The experience was affirming, and she is now successfully completing her first year as a psychology major.

Sense of Appreciation: Angela feels immersed in the coursework and feels the experience is taking her learning deeper and deeper. It all feels right, and she feels a deep sense of gratitude for this opportunity.

Sense of Purpose: Angela has a strong calling and connection to the field of psychology and often says: "I believe it picked me!"

Sensemaking: The ongoing coursework provides deeper and deeper layers of understanding and connections to her chosen field. It is also helping Angela make sense of the people that make up her world. She loves that her friends now count on her for relationship advice.

Clearly, this is a tale of two meanings. It is not difficult to see how each day would evolve for our two students. For Stephen, there is a large meaning void and, not surprisingly, the day often feels like a struggle, with recurring doubts about the major he selected. Angela has high levels of meaning across the board, and it reflects in the positive emotions she exhibits throughout the day.

The Parent Trap: Let's shift to a personal life example: parenting. Using the same framework, we see how parents might experience the role of parenting differently. Marie, a good friend of mine, is a great example. Her experience of meaning varies from low to high across the dimensions:

		Low	Med	High
Sense of Appreciation	Marie finds the experience of parenting to be inherently stressful and emotionally exhausting. Her demanding career creates ongoing challenges (and a lot of guilt) that she finds difficult to manage.	X		

		Low	Med	High
Sense of Purpose	Marie derives a great sense of purpose and value from being a parent. Her parents divorced when she was seven, and it has been her lifetime goal to create a stable family life for her kids.			X
Sensemaking	Marie tends to rely on her intuition in her parenting role and sometimes that doesn't work out. She would like to take a parenting class to enhance her skills.		X	

Clearly, parenting is a mixed experience for Marie. But these three categories provide a helpful framework she can leverage to enhance the meaning experienced in her parenting. While her sense of purpose is strong, there are certainly things she can do to raise her understanding of the challenges (e.g., parent support groups, classes, peer support, etc.). Her appreciation of the experience could be enhanced through mindfulness practices that allow her to be more fully present when needed.

Translating Meaning into "Everyday" Practices

Now that we are getting a feel for the *sources of meaning* in our lives, we shift our focus to creating the *kinds of practices* that will naturally create meaningful moments during the day. In the framework below, we translate the three sources of meaning into more specific practice areas relevant to *everydayness*.

Everydayness: Our Three Practices
Appreciation We create a unique *sensitivity, presence, and appreciation* for the diversity of moments that make the day uniquely ours. It starts by re-negotiating our relationship to time.
Purpose We bring a growing *sense of purpose* that greets us upon awakening each day and pulls us into the world with an engaging sense of direction and focus.
Sensemaking We cultivate a *sensemaking capacity* that allows us to thoughtfully deal with the unexpected, confusing, and emotional issues that can disrupt the flow of our day.

The framework only begins to define the three practice areas. In the next three chapters we will go deep in our exploration of each practice by revealing the routines and rituals that bring them to life. We will see how those routines and rituals provide stability in a chaotic world and become the essential pathways for finding that sense of wholeness we all long for.

Review and Reflect

Everydayness is an inner game. It reveals that many moments, when we are present to them, reveal a deeper pattern to our lives that we cannot risk missing. It acknowledges that our personal growth is not sudden or random but comes through a day-to-day attention that builds naturally. In fact, the only real way to combat the chaos, complexity, and busyness of our contemporary lives is by finding meaning in the moments that create both our routines and new experiences of the day.

Everydayness gives us our best chance to realize these aspirations.

St. Therese is an inspiring example! She dreamed of being a martyr and missionary who would travel to far-off lands, spreading her faith. But instead of a life of adventure and travel, she spent most of her short life in a cloistered convent, away from the outside world. She embraced what she called "the little way"—seeking holiness in the everyday moments of life and not in the grand gestures. We can certainly follow her lead when it comes to finding meaning in our days.

Chapter Two
Appreciation

Minding the moments

"This is the first, wildest, and wisest thing that I know—that the soul exists and is built entirely out of attentiveness."

— Mary Oliver

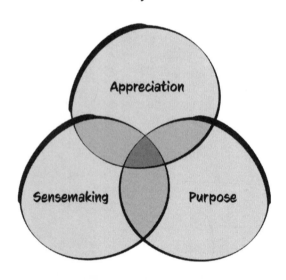

Key Themes	Questions We Will Answer
Appreciation as a Practice	*Why is "appreciating" essential to facilitating the kind of meaning we seek in our days?*
Your Attention Please	*How have "distraction" and "busyness" overtaken our lives?*
Minding the Moments	*How does the supporting practice of "minding the moments" serve as the everyday pathway to appreciation?*

The Practice of Appreciation

While I firmly believe *everydayness* is a powerful pathway to meaning-centered personal growth, it is important to remember that personal development is challenging, takes time, and is incremental in nature. Just think about any of your important growth journeys. Whether it was becoming a good parent, competent programmer, or competitive tennis player, the path was filled with ups and downs, progress and failure, and true tests of our patience and resilience. That's why our journey will be moment by moment and one day at a time.

This will take some discipline. As Americans we tend to measure our lives in terms of milestone events such as graduations, marriage, the birth of children, work promotions, and major holiday celebrations (including our birthdays). We use these milestones as important markers for a happy and meaningful life, as well as a source of the anticipative motivation for moving forward. For example, we may tell ourselves that we will be happy once we've gotten that promotion or have gotten married and have children. As a result, we live too much in the future, missing out on the here and now. Our *appreciating practice* will be our purposeful countermeasure, helping us access and create the kind of meaning that we can find each day.

To start our exploration, read the following three statements a couple of times and see to what degree you would agree with them. (Note: these questions are part of a *12-Question Everydayness Survey* that I use in my research).

1. I routinely slow to appreciate the simple moments of the day.

2. I can find some meaning in just about anything I experience.

3. Typically, I am fully present to the emotions I am experiencing.

These statements reflect our capacity to appreciate, value, and experience the world around us. As such, they represent one of our key sources of meaning in life. Admittedly, it was some time after midlife that I could even begin to appreciate these statements. Up until then, my work life was characterized by "rushing from one thing to the next" or "fitting one more thing in." I had fallen fully into the time management trap—thinking I could get everything done. In the pages that follow, we will explore how the artful practice of appreciating can help us stay connected, maintain a "newness in spirit" to what has become familiar, and open the door to new sources of meaning in our days.

This practice will also reveal how it is most often the small and easy-to-miss moments that can positively shape a day and a life.

These strategies are also well-supported by scholarly research. The father of meaning, Viktor Frankl, and a great number of contemporary "meaning researchers" have brought great validity to the notion that fully experiencing and valuing one's life experiences uniquely produces meaning in life.[7] As Frankl asserts, "Man not only finds his life meaningful through his deeds, his works, and his creativity, but also through his experiences."[8] This scholarly domain is known as Experiential Appreciation and has expanded our understanding of the traditional sources of meaning in life. It is often framed around achieving a sense of purpose and understanding in life.[9] As noted in chapter one, our *everydayness* practices build on these foundational sources.

> *"There is not one big cosmic meaning for all;*
> *there is only the meaning we each give to our life,*
> *an individual meaning, an individual plot, like an*
> *individual novel, a book for each person."*
> **— Anaïs Nin**

The bottom line is that fully experiencing life's moments, big and small, is one of the surest "everyday" pathways to living a fulfilling life. In fact, the practice of appreciating is also about learning to find meaning (albeit small) in just about every experience, whether it's savoring a meal with a friend or finding a new connection with a work colleague. *Everydayness* starts with the practice of appreciating because it opens the door to our complementary practices of *purpose* and *sensemaking* and allows us to be present in a world increasingly characterized by distraction and busyness. Instead of our lives passing by uneventfully, we learn to "slow down and show up" in our days in a much more intentional way. Thus, our simple definition of *appreciation*:

Appreciation is the practice of both experiencing and creating meaning from the wonderful range of moments, both good and bad, that make up our days.

Hopefully, the phrase "both good and bad" caught your attention. In our sensemaking practice (chapter four), we will explore how both the good and bad moments are what make our days rich in meaning. Even sadness (seemingly "bad") can produce a wide range of positive benefits that shape our inner lives in some extraordinary ways. But our focus for now is fully acknowledging that the moments of our days will require a level of attentiveness that has been lost in a world increasingly characterized by complexity and fragmentation. Let's dive into this formidable barrier.

Your Attention Please ...

Most of us are living what I call the *inattentive life*. This is easily symbolized by the centrality of smart phones in how we live and experience our lives (with our heads buried in these tiny screens). This is the new reality that has played out over the last two decades. Our phones are the first thing that greet us as we wake and the last thing we interact with before fading into the dark night. The smart phone (or any screen device) facilitates the messaging, requests, and expectations of endless others, which continually take precedence over our own thoughts and ideas.

And that's a problem.

With all the promise behind these twenty years of technological progress, we are left with the staggering and unintended result of our human experience being systematically fragmented and the sacred sense of the self increasingly undermined. We are not just overwhelmed by distractions, we increasingly seek them to "stay busy" as a way to reduce the pain, noise, and quiet suffering of our contemporary lives.

There is a real cost to our collective inattentiveness beyond the rising traffic deaths due to distracted drivers and the huge productivity losses in the workplace (measured in billions) caused by social media distractions.[10] There is also the well-documented evidence of how the overuse of social media time thwarts the academic achievement of our kids.[11] We didn't need a study to tell us that! Distraction has even entered our caring professions with reports of doctors doing internet searches during surgery and anesthesiologists logging into Facebook while monitoring your vitals! Here's what else we know about distraction:

- Distraction takes away the sense of flow and engagement of daily life, leaving us mired in an unsettling anxiety that follows us through the day.

- Distraction reduces our capacity for both deep thought and thoughtfulness, thereby reducing what it means to be truly human.

- Distraction causes us to rush to make up for the sense of "lost time"—with both mistakes and stress levels increasing as a result.

It shows up in both our personal and work lives, as acknowledged in the comments below:

Jill is a young professional and a planner in the marketing department of a major consumer brand. Jill and I met in one of my leadership workshops. She confided that

while all the busyness that comes with her role is energizing at times, it has its hidden costs as well. Jill shared
how a childhood best friend, Lynn, was in town for the
day and a special lunch was scheduled. Here is how Jill
described the lunch that she was fifteen minutes late for:

*"We had a couple of our usual dramas going on at work, and I
kept making excuses to check my phone for progress on the chaotic
threads that were going on back at work. I faked attention to
our conversation, but I know Lynn saw right through it. I was
barely in the room."*

Jill's story is a common one. In his recent book, *The World Beyond
Your Head*, Matthew Crawford refers to situations like these as
part of a world where "the effort to be fully present" is an ongoing struggle.[12] But beyond the challenge of being always on,
available, and connected, our attention and presence is undermined by another huge source of distraction:

Busyness.

Busyness

Busyness is often fueled by the constant handheld interruptions
that weave constantly through our days—even when perform-
ing surgery! What is the most popular response to the everyday
question, "How are you doing?"

"I'm soooooo busy."

Although exasperation is often feigned when making this response, there is also a sense of importance that comes with the "I'm so busy" disclosure. Busyness, you see, is a status symbol of sorts. After all, busy people are important and needed. In fact, we get so used to being busy that we have an aversion to idleness, inventing activities to keep us occupied. We even saw it in the pandemic, as we would stretch work and create unnecessary work to create the "busyness" that we got so used to.

In other words, busyness can be a distraction from what matters most. Busyness can also seem like the perfect response when we are avoiding emotional issues. If we can stay busy enough, the emotions can't break through and we won't have the opportunity to process the feelings that we are avoiding. As my friend Stephen reveals:

> *"Sometimes when I have a fight with my wife, I'm not ready to process things ... so I start cleaning the house like crazy. If friends come over and the house is super-clean, they know what that means."*

We may say that we have no "me time" but frequently we don't give ourselves that time because it can be painful and takes us places we aren't ready to go (like fully processing recent setbacks in work or relationships). Unfortunately, the loss of daily opportunities to check in with ourselves and do some meaningful reflection keeps us from becoming a growing, authentic, and guiding self.[13] When distraction and busyness prevail, we lose connection to the internal guidance system that keeps us true. As a result, our inner lives can feel less than whole and we are unable to participate fully in life, with most attention going to the "screens" in our life.

It is no wonder we are experiencing an epidemic of loneliness in our industrialized cultures, as our isolating and screen-driven worlds keep us from experiencing the wholeness of life. United States Surgeon General Dr. Vivek Murthy, in his book *Together: The Healing Power of Human Connection in a Sometimes Lonely World*, makes the case for loneliness as a public health concern and the source of increases in alcohol and drug abuse, violence, polarization, depression, and anxiety.[14] Proactively managing our attention is the first step in claiming our humanity and self-determination as human beings. Over and over and over again, we make one of the most important decisions we can make:

We choose what to pay attention to.

"Minding the Moments" Mindset

Shaping a new level of attentiveness is the solution to the dilemma of distraction and busyness—and we start by re-negotiating our relationship to time. Every day of our lives is filled with experiences and activities that we should relish, but which we quickly dismiss because we believe that we just don't have enough time. In other words …

Our lives are filled with blessings that we forget to count.

"Minding the moments" is a mindset that I have been integrating into all of my training sessions over the last fifteen years. Not only does it help participants stay out of the busyness trap, it reveals how the "quality of our attention" may be the most differentiating element in how we live our lives. That's worth a repeat:

The quality of our attention may be the most differentiating element in how we live our lives.

Here's the reality. We act as if there is simply not enough time, leading us to do lots of dumb things as we feel the pressure to be in action throughout the day. But what makes the "minding the moments" framing so impactful is that it allows us to rethink and renegotiate our sense of time. Researchers reveal that a moment is an actual unit of time: three seconds.[15] That's because three seconds is the minimal time it takes us to experience something. Let's count it out to fully appreciate the length of a moment:

one thousand one ... one thousand two ... one thousand three

As an example it may take about three seconds to realize that you are feeling tired. Or the grumbling in your stomach means you are hungry. And that flash of brilliance you get in the shower? It takes about three seconds to grasp this idea so you can quickly exit the shower and write it down! So, if a moment is three seconds, how many moments are there in a day? After subtracting eight hours for sleeping, the remaining sixteen hours translate into 20,000 waking moments every day. Let that sink in a bit.

When every new day rolls around, we have
20,000 moments at our disposal.

We also know that it takes just a few moments to make some-one's day, whether it be a compliment or a shared laugh. So, our first realization needs to be that we have plenty of time, even though we act as if we don't (rushing through things and poten-tially missing the uniqueness hidden in some of our moments). As we will see, it is not about trying to live each moment to the fullest. That would be exhausting! Our "minding the moments" mindset is about cultivating the kind of presence that moves us beyond the "busyness" that captures way too much of our days. It's not about managing time better, but rather it is a practice that seeks balance between …

being & doing.

One supporting ritual that gets to the heart of this "doing dilemma" is a timeless concept I learned during the pandemic: *Kairos*. It may be one of the most important words I have ever learned. The ancient Greeks had two words for time, *Chronos* and *Kairos*. *Chronos* time is best thought of as clock time. It's measurable and it is a big part of how we manage our days and live our lives. Since *Chronos* time is limited, we get consumed (and stressed!) trying to manage it.

Kairos time is measured not by a clock but by meaningful moments. We have to "slow down" to experience *Kairos* time. We can experience *Kairos* time at work when we slow to fully listen to a colleague or to fully unpack an emotion we are feeling.

Scientists may refer to *Kairos* time when they feel that a breakthrough in their thinking is emerging. An athlete would be in *Kairos* time when they feel time has slowed and, without expectation or pressure, they perform effortlessly. Theologians would define *Kairos* time as a time of contemplation, reflection, or prayer.

When I first introduced the concept of *Kairos* to my workshop participants, they got it right away. It gave them a concrete language to guide their thinking. Marie shares how she now leverages *Kairos* and *Chronos* as she shifts back and forth with her writing and daily routines:

> *"As an author, much of my day is spent writing, but I can only do it for so long (typically thirty to sixty minutes) before I need a break. I use this break time to not only refresh but to keep other parts of my life moving, like doing the dishes! Before I begin to write in the morning, I prepare to move into Kairos time by removing all the clutter from my desk and attending to any possible interruptions ... like a hungry cat."*

Over time, Marie has refined her writing ritual in some powerful ways that work for her. She continues her description:

> *"As I settle in to writing I remind myself I am now on Kairos time and the next thirty minutes shall not be interrupted as I turn over my thirty-minute hourglass. The passing sands are in partial view but just knowing they are there help me to focus. After each thirty-minute completion, I pause and check in to see if there is more in my tank."*

The important part of Marie's ritual is how she shifts her mind-set when switching to *Chronos* time:

> *"When I break from writing, I shift to my "to do" list. It is actually a welcome relief from the focus and discipline of putting sentences together. But before I start I remind myself I am now on "clock time" to get myself in the right mindset. Often I will block a time period ... like twenty minutes ... to keep me focused as I knock things off my list. I now feel good that my list is shorter (and the house is cleaner) and I am actually excited to return to the writing."*

Another benefit to embracing the *Kairos* spirit is that it can help us to anticipate potential *Kairos* moments as they emerge. Gabe, a new manager and workshop participant, had this to say:

> *"Yesterday I was a few minutes away from a meeting with a new staffer who was looking for some help on a project. My initial feeling was that this would be a distraction from my real work and would take some extra effort on my part. But luckily I caught myself being 'small Gabe.' It didn't feel good. In the moment, I reframed it as a great opportunity to help a fellow colleague. I had shifted into Kairos time."*

Beyond *Kairos*, I have introduced workshop participants to a range of "moment-centered" rituals that have been a part of my leadership and professional development practice over the last twenty years. These are time-tested "keepers" that are now deeply ingrained into the lives of hundreds of participants. The good news is that these supporting practices can be easily integrated into our day, cultivating a purposeful presence. But here's the challenge:

None of these rituals are possible without first pausing.

Pausing *is* the game changer. It is what makes "minding the moments" and *Kairos* work. It is what we learn to do first. We master it. It is the window to appreciating the moments, both mundane and magical. It is the essential part of the path to reclaiming our days. (Hundreds of workshop participants credit the "pause" as the essential element in their personal growth!) It is the simple practice that almost always precedes any kind of meaningful action. Pausing also promotes both a self-awareness and a mindful presence to the moments in our days as we experience them. So we pause. It takes just a moment:

one thousand one ... one thousand two ... one thousand three

Take one more moment for a deep breath. Maybe just one more. In just a few moments we start to feel a sense of calmness replace our amped-up physiology. The pause creates that necessary break between stimulus (a problem appears) and response (we take action). When we pause, we get the opportunity to choose. In just a moment or two we can discern that what we are about to do has real consequences. We feel the pressure to move forward, but pausing—just for a moment—gives us just enough mindful presence to keep our instinctive reactions in check. Not only does pausing help to relax and center us (giving our nervous system a needed break), it gives us options.[16]

How long should we pause? Well, it depends on the situation. The more emotional the issue, the longer the pause. The more complex the issue, the longer the pause. The more sensemaking that is needed, the longer the pause. In fact, a walk around the block may be needed to get some necessary distance from some issues. We also know that a good night's sleep will not only enhance our perspective but will often cut a problem in half!

For our *everydayness* approach, it is the little pauses throughout the day that become the focus of our "minding the moments" mindset. Here's the cool thing—we always get a little warning when it is time to pause. We feel it in our body. Imagine a colleague delivers a cutting remark about your proposal in a meeting. You feel your face become flushed, your sense of presence is shaken, and this feeling of anger starts to take control. So …

… we pause.

Consciously and deliberately pause whenever you get that "something is up" feeling. Remember, we often feel it first in our bodies or our emotions. If you are feeling rushed or a bit anxious, pause and take a deep "re-setting" breath. Repeat as necessary. If you are feeling stuck in your work, pause and walk around the block. If you are feeling a bit down, pause and count your blessings. Of course, the pause is what precedes your shifts between *Chronos* and *Kairos* time.

We pause often!

Pause and ... is the actual practice. Depending on the situation we learn to pause and _____. We fill in the blank with what is needed most. We want to make the pause a natural part of our day.

We pause ...

> ... and just breathe (we need a reset)
> ... and drop into Kairos time (to be fully present)
> ... and sip some tea (we need relief from the madness)
> ... and reframe the situation (it needs reframing!)
> ... and take a nap (just because)
> ... and take a walk (we need to get out of our heads)
> ... and call our moms (because moms know best).

You get the idea. Be creative and build a simple, meaningful "pausing" practice that works for you. There is no right or wrong way to do this.

Make it your own.

Pausing not only creates a neutralizing space between our actions, it also serves as a launch point for our practice of appreciation and the deeper rituals that bring it to life. One of the rituals that has made a big difference to our workshop participants over the years is the ritual of *savoring*. It is made possible by pausing and by the spirit of *Kairos*. It sits at the heart of appreciating and is the polar opposite of *being distracted*.

Savoring

Savoring is one of the most powerful responses to the distraction dilemma. Savoring is simply defined as appreciating and enhancing the positive experiences that occur in one's life. The cool thing is that we can savor the past, present, and future. Savoring the past is as simple as looking at family pictures from the last family holiday. We get to relive these precious moments again and again. Savoring the present is more about fully experiencing the current moment, whether it be that first cup of tea of the day or a favorite meal at lunchtime. We slow to a savoring pace to fully experience these moments. We can also savor the future by dreaming about an upcoming weekend event or a special vacation. One of my favorite savoring reflections came from a student in my MBA class, Ellen:

> *"I used to 'drink' my coffee in the morning. Now I savor every sip. I have found that sipping actually expands time ... and expands me."*

What comes forth are the positive emotions that put us in a good mood and provide a new source of energy for the day. David lives close to the beach and it has become his savoring "go to" for ending the day:

> *"It is impossible for me not to relax at the beach. I head there immediately after work. My hospital administration job is super stressful, but I am good at it and I feel needed. But I simply can't re-enter home life without some beach 'recovery' time. In my trunk I carry a beach towel and some comfy sweats that I*

quickly change into. The shoes immediately come off and the first sensation is toes in the sand as I head to the gently moving water line, where I begin my sacred walk.

As a start, I ask workshop participants to pick a daily routine, big or small, that they can use to intentionally build their savoring capabilities. It could be a morning coffee ritual or a child's bedtime story that you want to be fully present for. LeAnn used her after-work dog walk as her savoring experience. She would leave her phone at home and walk a local park path, delighting in being outdoors and with her best friend. Once you discover the magic of savoring, you will find yourself turning other routines into savoring rituals.

I leave you with my neighbor Anne's story:

Anne, a natural achiever, loved creating special moments for others. One such ritual was Saturday morning breakfast for the family, which included her five- and seven-year-old. A special menu was prepared with no details spared. The orange juice was hand squeezed. There was always the pressure to make the next breakfast better than the last. Over time, Anne realized that she was sitting at the edge of this morning ritual, observing but not fully participating. What once felt special now was starting to feel a bit like a burden. Anne started to scale back all the extra prep and earned a full and present seat at the table. Now Anne reveals: "I savor these moments we have together."

Review and Reflect

We live in an age of increasing anxiety and doubt as we struggle to create a coherent sense of self that will measure up to the demands and expectations of the world that surrounds us.[17] It is certainly not surprising that mindfulness as an appreciation ritual has moved into the mainstream, especially with the growing connections being revealed between our well-being and our ability to be present.[18]

We start our journey with the practice of appreciation because it sets the table for reclaiming our days. Rushing from one thing to another, we remain on the surface of life. Until we can learn to slow to a more present and purposeful pace, meaning-centered days will be elusive.

It starts with the acknowledgement that we have plenty of time once the moment becomes our unit of time for living our days. Twenty thousand moments roll into our account each day, providing an abundance of opportunities to experience and fully appreciate the life within and around us.

The capacity to fully appreciate is sustained by our ability to "be" in the moment, to be present. It is in this small safe harbor that reflection and renewal can be exercised daily so that we can weather the storms that characterize our post-pandemic world. It is our willingness to manage these moments that ultimately rewards us with a sense of clarity and focus that cannot be restrained.

one thousand one ... one thousand two ... one thousand three

"Our culture reasons that because we feel there is not enough time, we should increase our pace, multitask, and fit more into our already overbooked days. But even though it is counterintuitive to popular wisdom, perhaps the more effective response to the limits of time is to live more fully in the moment, to savor it and expand it."

– Carrie Newcomer

Chapter Three
Purpose

Doing things on purpose

"It's not about the destination; it's about the journey."
— Diana Nyad

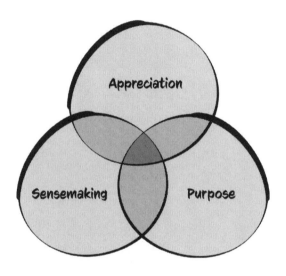

Key Themes	Questions We Will Answer
Exploring Purpose	*Why does our sense of purpose in life tend to emerge over time?*
"The Question"	*What would you be doing every day in your most meaningful life?*
Intention Setting	*How do we get full impact from our daily intentions?*

As you did for the *appreciating* practice in the last chapter, read the following three statements a couple of times and see to what degree you would agree with them.

1. I have a growing sense of purpose that guides how I live my days.
2. My days feel uniquely focused on the things that matter most.
3. I begin my days with an intentionality that brings out the best in me.

These statements reflect our capacity to be purposeful, the focus of our *purpose* practice. By developing a sense of purpose in life, we cultivate our true north, with each day being part of an emerging discovery process. I like the notion of true north because it points to an overall direction (like a compass) but doesn't tell you how to get there (like a navigation app). We have to find our own way.

With a growing sense of purpose, the self is continuously evolving and developing as we pursue the things that matter most. The benefits are significant. Having a strong sense of purpose is not only important to our well-being, both physical and psychological, but essential to our long-term human flourishing.[19] But let's consider the opposite for a moment.

What does it feel like when we don't have a sense of purpose in life?

Most likely, we have all been there at one point in our lives, experiencing the feelings of hopelessness, confusion, and anxiety. It can be a numbing feeling, unable to find enjoyment in *anything*. I can remember a "purpose-less" period in my own life where I struggled to get out of bed before noon. Feelings of emptiness would then follow me through the day as I grasped for any meaningful handhold.

A sense of purpose feels much different. It is that wonderful feeling that there is something very important that I am attending to—*and I am needed*. It is why we get up early. Cultivating a sense of purpose not only protects us from a lack of direction in life, it is especially important during the inevitable periods of transition when we seek new beginnings.

The Everydayness Journey

Everydayness is the journey we take to either find or live out a sense of purpose that is most relevant to us at this point in our lives. It is the daily progress on things that matter most that keeps us on the path. We may be called to a journey that represents our larger purpose in life. It's the young woman who has always dreamed of being a firefighter and is pursuing her dream with passion. That's wonderful when it happens but paradoxically and more importantly:

> *It is often the journey of finding our way in this world*
> *where a sense of purpose (often painstakingly) emerges.*

One of the questions that gets asked in my workshops is: *Where have you found the greatest sense of purpose and meaning in your work lives?* Anne, a wildly successful senior executive, made these thought-provoking comments:

> *"To this day the most meaningful job I ever had in my life was shoveling horse crap, often in the freezing winter. It was my job to help pay my way through college. I came to the stalls in the late afternoon after classes. It was just me and the horses and this quiet time was a perfect way for me to end the day. It started as a meaningless job, but over time it felt like me and my new friends were sensing and honoring each other's existence as I cleaned their stalls before they turned in for the night.*

> *"I had never ridden a horse but it felt special to be around these majestic beasts. Nothing rivals the feeling when a horse approaches you on their own ... wanting to be in your presence. I also loved the physical nature of the work ... it made me feel like I was actually doing something. My last day at the stalls, after almost two years, was extremely hard. It was saying goodbye to these horses ... which I named and now knew deeply.*

> *"Over time I discovered that I loved them more than anything else in my life. I cried ... no, I sobbed the whole way home that last night. I also realized I was also saying goodbye to the surprisingly purposeful patterns that evolved in my work ... and more surprisingly brought great meaning to my life. This experience thirty years ago has led to the only career advice I give ... .*

> *"Sometimes you gotta shovel sh*t to find your place in the world."*

I love Anne's response because it brings purpose and meaning down to ground level. Similar to Anne, I have experienced hospital cleaners and others in seemingly undesirable jobs who actually see their work as noble, fulfilling, and purposeful. As previously noted, Frankl's Holocaust experience and subsequent research reveals that it is our natural "will to meaning" that allows us to find a sense of purpose in these unusual places. In other words, it is less about the work itself and more about our internal desire to make a difference … to find meaning … so we find a way.

What we know for sure is that the purpose we find in life will be unique for each of us and will undoubtedly shift through life as we evolve and grow from new experiences—and respond to a world that may need us in some dramatically different ways. We love stories that begin with … *"From my earliest memories, I always knew I wanted to be (fill in the blank)."* Unfortunately, these responses give the impression that our purpose is deep and already within us. That's cool when it happens but, for most of us, purpose in life is *cultivated* out of the things that are most meaningful to us and discovered in our everyday lives. It is also through our everyday lives that we confirm these aspirations over time. Ellen, a workshop participant, shared these reflections:

> *"My mom was an activist. I grew up dirt poor but also learned to deeply empathize with others like me. I got my law degree so I could represent those who need it most. That is now my life."*

Ellen's sense of purpose was not experienced as a one-time epiphany but reflects a lifelong experience that cultivated a deep sense of service for the underserved in her community. In other words, our purpose doesn't start with what we are good at but rather with what is important to us … *what we value.*

My real estate friend, LuAnne, claims it took her two decades to cultivate a sense of purpose around her work. She got her license after her husband left her with two small kids at home. Non-degreed, LuAnne felt her career options were limited and real estate seemed like her best chance to bring financial stability to her family. In her words:

> *"Initially I was motivated by sheer survival and thank God I had some early success. I was always a top producer in my office, mostly due to the fact that I worked the hardest. I didn't like the long hours, but I loved the independence and the ability to provide a secure life for my kids. Slowly but surely the game changed from 'number of deals done' and 'awards on the wall' to what felt like a 'personal practice' that went way beyond the sales transaction. I found myself helping clients find the right schools for their kids or plan a remodel. These activities often occurred long after the sale! I discovered that I loved helping, and it created a new and special relationship to my work and my clients … with many becoming close friends."*

LuAnne's story is both down-to-earth and compelling. Growing our sense of purpose seeks to cultivate this kind of meaning-finding. Our approach starts with a simple but essential question:

> *What would you be doing every day in*
> *your most meaningful life?*

(Note: I have intentionally stayed away from conceptual questions like: *What is your purpose in life?*" These framings can feel too broad and a bit intimidating to many of us—and simply won't work in a world where we may have to reinvent ourselves multiple times over a lifetime. The question may also give the limiting impression that we have only one purpose in life that remains consistent.)

For my friend LuAnne, her answer to this question is now simple: *Helping people find a house and then make it their home.* What makes this question work are two key phrases: "doing every day" and "most meaningful." Probably nothing reveals our sense of purpose than something we would want to do every day and also provides the most meaning to us. The answer to this question actually flows quite easily. Here are some sample responses:

> *"It's building a great family life for our three kids. I work part-time because we need the money but family is where my priorities are." Steve*

> *"It's my cancer research ... and I can get lost in it. More than science, I love learning. The opportunity to go deep in discovery with the potential for a breakthrough takes over my waking hours." Taylor*

> *"For me, everything I do involves fashion in some way. I am still figuring out what my work will look like but, believe me, it will involve fashion." Hope*

As you can see, there are a range of responses from "family" to "professional pursuits" to "passionate endeavors." All are certainly valid, and our *everydayness* strategy would honor each unique purpose. In all of the examples above, it is important to note that it is something beyond a job or career that gets identified. This is key. Feeling a sense of purpose comes from the deeper well of serving something larger than ourselves. As Frankl discovered, it is this bigger pursuit that makes life worth living.[20] Later in our discussion we will reveal the key elements that give our sense of purpose the stability of true process. But first we gain clarity on our key question that captures our purpose in life:

> *What would you be doing every day in*
> *your most meaningful life?*

Of course, as you grow and the world around you changes, your answer will change. That's a good thing. We just can't set it and forget it. We have to work it. As you read through the three simple examples above, try out your response. It may involve your current job or it may not.

See if you can write your overarching purpose in ten words or less, keying in on the phrase "doing every day in my most meaningful life." Getting it out of our head and onto paper can be a clarifying process. We will leave the empty box below as a reminder and placeholder for your response:

This process has also been helpful in recultivating a sense of purpose for those whose jobs have become routine over time. Whether it be teachers, flight attendants, accountants, or nurses, work can become dull and too familiar, losing its motivating spark. Amazingly, having people reflect on how it felt when they first began can restart the purposing process. As one of our workshop participants, Liz, reflected:

> *"When I first got into teaching, I didn't believe I could change the world, but I did believe I could have a positive impact on these little lives that were entrusted to me for a school year. Much of that energy has faded with time and the challenges of working in a grossly under-resourced profession. I am working to get that energy back."*

Everydayness is about living our purpose every day in both small and big ways. If you are lucky, the thing that you love doing most is a big part of your day. It may even be your job. Or it may be something you fight to find time for. Think of the actor who works two survival jobs while taking night classes, practicing with an "improv" group, and going on countless auditions.

We also know that it may take time (possibly a lifetime) to fully discover how to put our passions and sense of purpose into play. We also may find ourselves on the wrong path.

Two years ago, I was coaching a mid-career professional, Tim. He had left a highly stable and successful manager role to join a prestigious consulting firm where a good friend worked. The transition from managing a small operations team to leading complex change projects was a nightmare for Tim. Nothing in his previous roles prepared him for the chaotic consulting world. In fact, there was little in the new role that he liked. More than anything, he was troubled by how he could have made such a bad career decision. Not surprisingly, much of our time together was soul-searching that question.

Like Tim, many of us have had the experience of following a false pursuit that would satisfy our ego and look good to others only to find that our true self was not aligned. It is common wisdom that somewhere around 50% of all college graduates think they picked the wrong major. Some of the reason may be due to a lack of life experience, but a lot of it is due to the huge influences of the "small world" we live in (e.g., family, friends, etc.) and the "larger world" of popular culture that highlights (often through social media) what is most important. As a result ...

We can get lost.

It is easy to see how we can lose connection with our true selves as we conform to who we think we should be rather than who we are. We are molded as children by our parents, teachers, clergy, friends, peers, and the larger culture to "fit in"—to be a true team player. As a result, we developed beliefs, thoughts, feelings, and behaviors that kept us acting in ways that weren't always developed from within. We learned to *adapt* to these external influences and pressures.[21] Cultivating a true sense of purpose over time helps to counter these external pressures.

Purpose as an Everyday Process

Remember, purpose is the everyday pursuit of what matters most in our life, shaping what we do and who we will become. Workshop participants have consistently pointed to daily "intention setting" as having the greatest impact on this process. It starts with the humbling realization that the one thing we have most control over is *how we begin the day*. Everything else proceeds at the whims of a chaotic world that we live and work in.

Our workshop participants also discovered that letting their typically over-scheduled days just evolve did not compare to the feelings generated when priority intentions were in play. Just the act of setting intentions produced powerful feelings of self-determination.

Let's start our exploration by defining what we mean by "daily intentions." Most of us have three main "boxes" where we develop our direction in life. Our long-term goals and aspirations establish an overall course, serving as the markers that we want to make progress toward. These bigger goals come to life as they are broken down into meaningful and specific milestones that we can target and plan around more specifically. This first box could also include dreams and aspirations that we are nurturing.

With the clarity of goals, we can start building our to-do lists (which can include our more detailed plans for our projects). Most of us maintain multiple lists that represent the different parts of our lives (e.g., personal, work, special projects, etc.). The wonderful thing about to-do lists is that they give us a sense of control in our complex, ever-changing lives. Once I get a new item onto one of my lists, it relieves the immediate burden of taking some kind of action because … *"it's on the list and I can stop worrying about it for now!"*

The third box is our daily intentions—the items we will prioritize for the day. These intentions can be carefully sourced from our to-do lists and will vary in their degree of detail and specificity (with some examples below). But here's an important pause point. We need to develop these daily intentions wisely because it is our intentions that will significantly determine three things:

1. How our sense of purpose will grow.

2. What gets done.

3. Who we will become.

It is easy to see why intention setting is central to our *everydayness* practice. I agree with the previous quote from Annie Dillard that it is how we live our days that determines our lives. But I also believe it is our intentions that determine the impact of our days.

Here's the intention-setting practice that I have leveraged over the last ten years. (In other words, I have done it over 3,000 times!) It is one of the main reasons I was inspired to write this

book. It starts with a line in the middle
of a blank page. Above the line I write
one to three priority intentions (I never
have more than three.) They answer the
simple question: *What are the intentions I will
prioritize for today?* These are the intentions
that matter most and gain the special status

of being above the line. Below the line are other intentions that
I hope to get done, but I don't let them interfere with the top
priorities. They may have to wait until tomorrow. Here's where
it gets interesting:

I complete the above-the-line intentions over 90% of the time.

Not only does this completion rate provide a powerful sense
of accomplishment for the day, it gives me the confidence that
what I decide to prioritize will get done. Clearly, much of the
success rate has to do with the focus on just a few priorities. Plus,
my sense of success for the day is not built around how much
is done but by making progress on what matters most. That's
worth a pause. Instead of feeling overwhelmed by the number
of things not done on the list, I am feeling great about how the
important things are consistently getting done.

Here's the other secret behind the success. (It's definitely not
some amazing level of discipline or focus that I have!) The secret
is linked to a special part of the brain, the reticular activating
system (RAS). It's the RAS that helps us to organize information in powerful ways. It starts by filtering out unnecessary

information so that the important stuff gets through—like our priority goals.

The RAS is the reason that when you learn a new word, it starts popping up everywhere. It's why tire stores that you haven't noticed before start emerging when you need tires. Whatever you make a priority, the RAS creates a filter for. Amazing, right? It gets better. The RAS does all of this automatically, without us noticing or having to make any extra effort. It is continually and actively working on the things that are most important to us. You couldn't hire a more capable assistant.

When I go through the process of confirming my one to three priorities for the day, my RAS is taking special note. It is now "programmed" to begin revealing the information, people, and other potential opportunities that will bring these goals to life. To fully turn on these resources, I spend a few extra moments in *Kairos* time locking in my priority intentions, often visualizing the outcomes I am looking for. For example, if I am leading a workshop that day, I will set specific intentions to promote its success.

With my priority intentions set, I now shift to other important intentions that I place below the line. Because I am consistently reviewing and updating my to-do lists, these items are also well known to my RAS and almost always get done as well. The cool thing is that the RAS will still make a special effort to protect the above-the-line intentions—hence, my incredible success rate.

Here's a side-bar story I love telling. When my parents retired, I set (and routinely reaffirmed) a special intention to do all that I could to make their retirement a special one. My RAS was all in and delivered opportunities over and over again. Here's an example: At the end of a ski season in Big Sky, Montana, I had some extra passes that I was going to give away to some lucky stranger. Seemingly out of the blue (thank you RAS!) I remembered that these passes could be exchanged for summer golf passes. My parents, who love golf, were treated to a three-day golf excursion!

As you can see, the RAS is naturally aware of the things I value most. It also serves as a vigilant gatekeeper. So, wherever I find meaning and purpose, my RAS will take note and 1) help me make new connections that are aligned and 2) filter out things that are not. When I was writing this book, all kinds of incredible resources revealed themselves (e.g., ideas, articles, LinkedIn connections, etc.) without any special effort on my part. For example, many articles are "pushed" to me from research sites I subscribe to. While I find myself quickly deleting many of these "pushes" because at first blush they don't seem to fit, the RAS will slow me down as if to say, *"You may want to take a second look at this one."* I am often rewarded with a breakthrough idea.

That's the power of the RAS. But let's be clear. If we don't set intentions in advance (which could be the night before), our daily lives will lose ground to the always-present urgencies and curveballs of the day. Here are some illustrative examples of intentions from fellow colleagues:

Taylor, our cancer researcher, has crafted one important intention for the day: *Complete and distribute my research paper identifying a potential new discovery path.*

For LuAnn, our "house to home" realtor, her purpose-related intention for the day is: *Start a resource guide of local and trusted home repair techs.*

Liz, our school teacher, seeks to revitalize her sense of purpose. One of her daily intensions that she uses routinely is: *Make sure each student feels seen today.* A new intention is: *Explore more small-group activities, starting today.*

Steve, a stay-at-home dad, has committed to this intention: *Practice being more fully present (which has fallen off lately) when interacting with the kids.*

When we shape and commit to these intentions, they have the power to bring our emerging sense of purpose to life. Plus, as these intentions build on a daily basis, they create a powerful and compounding snowball effect. In other words, our priority intentions today will often build on our intentions from yesterday and undoubtedly help to grow our intentions for tomorrow. Here's a critical pause point. Many of our above-the-line intentions, representing our most important efforts, are rarely once and done.

For example, when writing this book, most of my above-the-line intentions focused solely on making progress on the book. With only a 90-day window to complete it, I simply could not let anything else get in the way. In fact, my loyalty to the project was so intense, I would "without guilt" forego other important priorities for the day, including exercise (which sometimes downshifted into a walk around the neighborhood as a needed break from writing). This was easy for me because, of all the things I do in my work, none of them brings a sense of meaning to my days like writing. Here's an example of the first two intentions I set (and recorded in my notebook) on the day I started this book:

- Complete an initial outline for the book.
- Begin shaping an "introduction" that creates a compelling overview of the book.

In response to these intentions, I was able to create an overall outline, but it definitely needed some refinement. I was also able to start writing an introduction. I remember actually starting two different themes for the intro that I wanted to test. The next day, my new intentions reflected this progress and the need to build on these efforts. I also added a third intention to start getting feedback on the proposed title.

- Complete a second pass on the overall outline for the book, adding sub-headings for each chapter.
- Complete a first draft of the "pandemic version" of the introduction.
- Test the working title of *Everydayness* with family and friends.

I use the simple visual of yesterday, today, and tomorrow to symbolize how we can build and grow our intentions day by day. Without letting the separation of time disrupt our momentum, we carefully "stitch" our days together. As our intentions grow in a purposeful direction, so do we.

In my example above, a key project became the focal point for my daily intentions for a three-month period. You may find yourself in intense project periods as well, where a singular focus may prevail. But most of us will also experience periods of time where our priorities are more short-term in nature. Here are a few illustrative examples:

- Making a solid start on a new job
- Making progress on finding a new apartment
- Stabilizing the "homework routine" for the kids

While some of these intention themes may not bring your sense of purpose to life, they may truly reflect your current "top-of-line" priorities. Making consistent progress will undoubtedly make the day feel "purposeful." In other words, submitting our taxes on time may relieve that sense of burden that has been creeping into our days and free us up for meaningful priorities. Yes, my friends, tackling the mundane can feel great!

The reality is that most people will have good intentions for the day, but not always follow through. With *everydayness*, our aim is to live *intentionally*, making progress consistently on the things that matter most. Dropping into *Kairos* time (which can take a few moments) ensures that we don't rush and can fully focus on setting the right intentions for the day. With consistent and ongoing completion of our intentions, our days can feel uniquely purposeful, despite the inevitable detours, distractions, and low points.

Review and Reflect

I love the subtitle for this chapter: *Doing things on purpose*. It's a simple play on words, but it gets to the heart of the *everydayness*. Our busy days are filled with "doing" and at times very little of it may relate to the underlying meaning and purpose in our lives. In short, we need to be doing more things *on purpose*.

It starts with cultivating a sense of purpose that will be unique to us. For most of us, this will take some time and will be hard-earned through both wins and losses. (Paradoxically, the losses often teach us the most.) Since *everydayness* emphasizes the things we do every day, we brought our purpose-finding down to ground level with the question:

> *What would you be doing every day in*
> *your most meaningful life?*

I am always asking this question and it always engenders a uniquely interesting response. With a sense of purpose emerging we can start our daily journey in earnest. We then discovered it is through intention setting that our days become a true and defining force in our lives.

Instead of relying on discipline or extra effort (good luck with that!), we turn on an intensely intuitive and powerful part of the brain (the RAS) that will work around the clock to ensure that our priorities and their envisioned progress will happen. I am delighted to affirm that the RAS is an internal resource, a natural part of who we are.

In the first chapter, I warned that we are living in a world where we must increasingly accept that we alone play the dominant role in shaping our lives. Our emerging sense of purpose and supporting intention-setting practice confirms ...

We got this!

Chapter Four
Sensemaking

Slowing to the speed of thoughtfulness

*"Never doubt that a small group of thoughtful,
committed individuals can change the world.
In fact, it's the only thing that ever has."*

— Margaret Mead

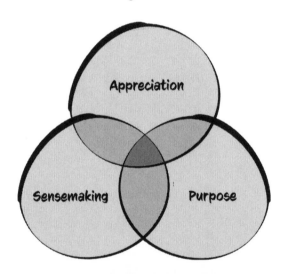

Key Themes	Questions We Will Answer
Sensemaking	*How does sensemaking promote meaning and understanding in our lives?*
Thoughtful Sensemaking	*Why is "thoughtfulness" the perfect principle for our sensemaking efforts?*
The Paradoxical Power of Sadness	*What important role do emotions play in facilitating our "everyday" sensemaking?*
Pause and Reframe	*How does the power of the pause keep us "open" for business?*

Here is what we have discovered so far. *Appreciation* is being present to the meaningful moments of the day by cultivating a new relationship to time and our capacity to being attentive. *Purpose* is bringing our deeper sense of purpose into our days—not letting what matters most get lost in our tomorrows. Our third and final practice area, *sensemaking*, is the critical meaning-making process for how we deal with the unexpected, confusing, and emotional issues that can disrupt the flow of our day. When combined, these three practices allow us to live our days (and hence our lives) in the most fulfilling way.

As we did for the *appreciating* and *purposing* practices, read the following three statements a few times and see to what degree you would agree with them.

1. I spend the necessary time "making sense" out of disruptions that occur during the day.

2. I slow to a more thoughtful pace when the situation calls for it.

3. I am known for effectively managing the inevitable negative emotions we all experience daily.

It is through sensemaking that we can respond fully to the inevitable challenges that occur every day and can take us off course. We have all probably had a situation similar to Linda's, where a whole day might be lost because of one small incident. Here's what happened:

Linda is super excited about tomorrow. She has blocked off ninety minutes at work to spend on her passion project.

She rarely gets this much time to focus on anything. With morning time blocked out, she anticipates great progress. Unfortunately, shortly after arriving to work she receives one of those zinger e-mails. Joe, a colleague from another department, has sent out a project update that has grossly mischaracterized Linda's recent activity. Linda is upset. No, Linda is angry. She immediately dives into drafting a "correcting" e-mail. Her first version is overly terse, so she spends time toning down a new draft. Unfortunately, the sent version starts a flurry of e-mails from different respondents. E-mail "hell" is fully underway, and Linda's ninety minutes of precious project time is lost … making her even more upset. Although the communications are corrected to Linda's satisfaction, the emotional fallout follows her through the day as she finds herself continually ruminating over the morning mishap.

Here is how her story ends.

It took more than a few long walks over the weekend before Linda could finally put it to bed. But it came with the realization that she didn't have to respond to the zinger e-mail right away. She didn't have to lose the personal time that she blocked. *She could have made a better choice.*

Sensemaking is a practice that not only helps us to make sense out of things, it helps us to manage our feelings and make better choices. How do we respond when …

The data in the report doesn't make sense.
A sick child interrupts our intended schedule for the day.
A colleague fails to deliver promised information ... again.
A small mistake I just made could have significant impacts.
We fret on how to best recover from an overreaction with a
family member.

Remember, our first reaction to any event is almost always emotional ... not neutral or rational. Let's look at the list above one more time with a possible emotion that would be experienced first in ALL CAPS.

The data in the report doesn't make sense. I AM CONFUSED

A sick child interrupts our intended schedule for the day.
I AM ANXIOUS

A colleague fails to deliver promised information ... again.
I AM ANGRY

A small mistake I just made could have significant impacts on
others. I AM FEARFUL

We fret on how to best recover from an overreaction with a
family member. I AM FEELING GUILTY

Because emotions happen automatically, we have to intentionally manage them. Imagine how Linda's day might have turned out if she had not overreacted to the e-mail. Imagine if she got her ninety minutes of uninterrupted time for her special project. The resulting progress and sense of control would have undoubtedly shaped a much more positive day. As we can see, how we respond to our emotions, especially when experiencing time pressures, is critical. Not only is the flow of the day at risk but so is our well-being. We start with this realization: Much of the sensemaking we do on a daily basis is driven by emotions. As we shall see, that is not necessarily a bad thing. We also start with this acknowledgement:

Emotions can grab our attention like nothing else.

In other words, when there is a disruption to *what we do* or *who we are*, our emotions are elevated. We can become excited or fearful. Hopeful or disillusioned. This is one of our critical pause points throughout our journey because we still tend to see emotions as something to be suppressed or managed. My view is the opposite:

Emotions need to be seen as a fundamental part of our efforts to make sense of the world that surrounds us.

In fact, being human is characterized by experiencing emotions in ways that can help us. Sadness elicits empathy and can draw in social support when it is needed most. Anxiety alerts us to potential threats that mean we should proceed with caution. Anger can mobilize us to necessary actions that might be out of our comfort zone. Emotions also help us to interpret what is "truly going on" as we sort through and make sense out of our feelings.

For example, a "gnawing feeling" followed me to my car after a recent meeting. Instead of starting the car I sat with these feelings, which soon emerged as a question to me: *Was the meeting too much about my ideas?* A little more reflection revealed that the answer was "yes." In hindsight, I was overreacting to the time limits of the meeting … feeling the pressure to get my ideas out. A brief note of apology was sent to the meeting participants, with returning notes of appreciation from these colleagues.

The Paradoxical Power of Sadness

Let's continue our discussion with a deeper dive into the special teaching and healing qualities of sadness, one of the most common emotions experienced in our lives. It is an emotional state of unhappiness, ranging in intensity from mild to extreme and usually aroused by the loss of something. While sadness is often considered a negative emotion, it serves an important role in signaling a need to receive help in some way.

Sadness also helps us to pause and slow down. It encourages us to reflect, to look inward as we explore our feelings. When we experience sadness, it can also create a sensitivity to the sadness others are experiencing. It is no surprise that losses, big and small, surround us. Probably on a daily basis, someone in our close orbit needs some empathy or support. It could be us. Paradoxically, it is in these moments that we often find opportunities for our own personal development and growth.

Sammie didn't get the job that she had been working so hard for. Deep disappointment and feelings of discouragement followed her for the next few days. But soon time gave way to some needed soul-searching (and a few "best friend" chats) that allowed Sammie to acknowledge that this wasn't her time and more prep was needed. A new sense of commitment and hope emerged as Sammie began to fully prepare for the next opening.

As with Sammie, emotions can signal that we need to rethink and reframe things as we try to create new meanings that will propel us forward. More than anything, our emotions serve as a needed interruption to the normal, almost automatic nature of our daily routines or practices. When things get emotional, energy mobilizes and attention becomes focused. When we step outside of our normal routines and comfort zones, the opportunity for personal growth and creativity occurs. In other words:

We can benefit from the emotional interruption!

Here's the good news. A powerful approach to sensemaking (especially in our emotion-driven days) has been developed and continually refined over the last two decades in my professional and leadership development workshops. It connects people to the power of emotions in our everyday lives and is built on the uniquely generative principle of *thoughtfulness.*

Thoughtful Sensemaking

What I have learned most deeply in working with a broad range of individuals and organizations is that *thoughtfulness*, when present, dramatically impacts how we interact with others. This is especially true in our work lives. It gives us the feeling that we are not just reacting to some challenge but responding in a meaningful way. Here's why. In our "just do it" lives, preference is mostly given to action-oriented and knowing behaviors. As a result, we can easily lose sight of others. We communicate with them but don't connect. We inform them but fail to fully involve them. Here's the real challenge:

> The emotional complexities in our post-pandemic lives continue to increase as our emotional intelligence and related capabilities continue to lag.

In response, I have consistently witnessed how the practice of "thoughtful sensemaking" creates a powerful pathway to build the kind of emotional competence that is needed. As the complexity and pace of change in our work lives intensify, we will all need to become more aware of how emotions can either facilitate or undermine both our individual and collective efforts. To fully understand the practice of thoughtful sensemaking, let's start by understanding how others perceive the importance of being *thoughtful*.

In one of my workshop exercises, hundreds of participants have been given thirty-two cards representing a healthy range of admirable traits that we would like to see in ourselves and others.

Those traits are listed below. Typically, I ask them to think of what characteristics they would want most in a colleague or a supervisor in their organization. The card sort goes through three rounds where I ask them to successively keep only half of the cards that describe the desired characteristics best. Each round only takes about five minutes to complete the card sort. Here's how it goes.

Round One: Reduce the thirty-two cards to sixteen cards.

Round Two: Reduce the remaining sixteen cards to eight cards.

Round Three: Reduce the remaining eight cards to four cards.

With this last card sort, participants now have just four cards in front of them that get to the heart of what they would want most in a colleague or supervisor. Here's what I discovered. The word "thoughtful" almost always made the final four—no matter the type of work environment (e.g., financial, health care, manufacturing , service, etc.). No other word came close. Initially I was surprised, thinking that bolder words like "courageous" or "competent" would be chosen more often. I was motivated to dig deeper.

Communicator	Accountable	Self-Aware	Driven
Courageous	Confident	Empathic	High Integrity
Strategic	Commanding	Patient	Competent

Loyal	Visionary	Thoughtful	Inspiring
Committed	Respectful	Responsible	Helpful
Focused	Intelligent	Selfless	Transparent
Relational	Trustworthy	Resilient	Compassionate
Hopeful	Energetic	Creative	Curious

In debriefing with workshop participants, I found that the word *thoughtful* resonated for a couple of key reasons. Whether it was a colleague or supervisor, they wanted someone they could truly collaborate with, not someone driving their own success. *Thoughtful* also conveyed the sense of caring that many wanted to experience in their work. As Tory revealed:

"With all the stretch goals and endless targets, we have lost our capacity to empathize–with our customers, and with each other."

My interest and research continued. I found that thoughtfulness actually has two meanings, both pointing to character traits.[22] **Meaning 1** relates to the sensemaking or the deeper thinking and discipline we might bring to an issue (e.g., she was thoughtful in her writing). **Meaning 2** relates to how we relate to others in positive ways (e.g., more than kind, he brought a special thoughtfulness to his dealings with others). It also suggests a sense of compassion toward others. Finally, there seems to be a "permanence" to the word thoughtful, with our tendency to use it as a sign of character, not a fleeting behavior. Most notable to me was the finding that when we experience compassion, all kinds of benefits accrue, including the reduction of stress, enhanced personal growth, and the development of trust with others.

> *"If there were one word that could act as a standard of conduct for one's entire life, perhaps it would be thoughtfulness."*
> — **Confucius**

With its dual focus on deeper thinking and compassion, *thoughtful* became the perfect descriptor for our sensemaking practice. Most importantly, it acknowledges the influence of emotions on sensemaking. This is a critical pause point. As reinforced a few times already, we initially experience events emotionally, and our capacity to manage these feelings is what keeps our days in flow. The "thoughtful sensemaking" framing reinforces this vital relationship between sensemaking and emotions, a relationship that is essential to living our days more fully.

So how do we effectively manage the feelings that are so intertwined with our sensemaking efforts? I will take you through a typical workshop exercise and exploration to bring "thoughtful sensemaking" to life. Let's dive in.

Thoughtful Sensemaking Exercise:

It starts with a simple question that helps to break the ice in the room:

> *Has anyone here ever felt ... left out ... embarrassed ... overlooked ... not appreciated ... underutilized ... overwhelmed ... confused ... burnt out?*

The hands go way up as we all enjoy a laugh together, realizing that these are fairly normal and often everyday occurrences. While these feelings may be normal, we still need to manage them well.

In phase two of the exercise, we acknowledge that we sometimes react negatively to our felt emotions. I share ten possible reactions (see below) to get the juices flowing. I share my typical negative reactions first and then invite others to share as well. I tend to withdraw and obsess—a wonderful combination! Participants actually have fun revealing their typical reaction when they are not at their best. After all, we're human.

• *Overreacting*	• *Getting angry*
• *Blaming others or self*	• *Becoming defensive*
• *Withdrawing*	• *Becoming aggressive*
• *Obsessing over it*	• *Holding a grudge*
• *Becoming anxious*	• *Other reactions!*

In phase three of the exercise, we get to share our strategies for responding to negative emotions when we are *at our best*. Again, I show ten potential actions (which they can add to), and we share the go-to strategies that seem to work best for us. I start by sharing that I tend to be good at staying positive and problem-solving when emotions are running high (particularly my own). Participants are also excited to share the strategies that work best for them.

• *Reframe the situation*	• *Take action*
• *Accept the situation*	• *Gain understanding*
• *See the positive*	• *Be resilient*
• *Forgive and forget*	• *Problem-solve*
• *Remain open*	• *Get creative*

You may be starting to see the learning tension I am trying to create. First of all, negative emotions are a "given" in this crazy world, but as we saw in the exercise, our response can be negative or positive. (Although we may wish to remain neutral, neutrality is rarely an option when emotions are at play.) At this point I underscore for the workshop participants that our response is a choice. We get to choose how we manage our feelings. It is not always easy but, as in the case of Linda's lost day, we always have a choice. It is supported by a simple meme:

We experience our emotions automatically but
manage our feelings intentionally.

This is where the discussion gets interesting for workshop participants. I reinforce that at any given moment we are either "open" or "closed" in terms of our true availability to ourselves and others. When negative feelings are at play, we close down. When positive feelings are being experienced, we open up. In the framework below I use a simple "open for business" metaphor to differentiate between the two. Here's how I do it.

In the workshops I show both signs that we have become accustomed to seeing (open and closed for business) and gain participant concurrence that we instinctively look for these signs as we approach businesses—especially those that are new to us. We want that affirmation that they are open, ready to welcome us. I ask the simple question: How does it feel when you approach a new coffee shop or lunch place recommended by a friend and you see the "open" sign in the window? Not surprisingly, all kinds of positive feelings are felt. Conversely, how does it make you feel when you see the closed sign as you get closer to the door? Of course, feelings of disappointment are expressed. The same goes for us personally. Sometimes we have the "open for business" sign out … welcoming others in. At other times, we are communicating (even non-verbally) that we are not open for business. It is often because we are in the grip of some kind of negative feeling.

In the framework below I reveal how "open" and "closed" can show up in our personal lives as we relate to and connect with others.

Open for Business	Closed for Business
I am accessible.	I am not accessible.
I welcome you.	I am distracted.
I can relate to you.	I am not ready to relate to you.

This framing always promotes some soul-searching because deep down we all know that when we are actively engaged in this chaotic and uncertain world, we are often toggling between being "open" and "closed" for business. The follow-up questions I pose are:

How do we keep the "open for business" sign on when the inevitable negative feelings occur?

How do we make better choices when emotions are running high and we can feel them taking over our bodies?

In other words, how do we ensure our emotions don't take us down the wrong path prematurely? I can't reinforce this next point enough:

Our best response to any challenging situation always starts with a "pause."

Pausing was introduced in chapter two as a critical gateway to *appreciating*, and it serves the same important role in *sensemaking*. Pausing gives us needed separation from the emotion-causing stimulus (and just about everything creates some kind of emotional response). Pausing gets our hyped-up nervous system back to neutral (or at least out of the red zone). We can start to be more objective … more rational. How long do we pause? It might be just a couple of moments for a minor disturbance or the benefit of a good night's sleep for a failure at work.

The general rules of thumb from chapter two are repeated in the workshop:

The more emotional the issue, the longer the pause.
The more complex the issue, the longer the pause.
The more sensemaking that is needed, the longer the pause.

Participants also begin to plan "pausing" rituals that would personally work for them. They are encouraged to think of the pause as a positive distraction as they:

Pause and breathe.
Pause and sip some tea.
Pause and take a walk around the block.
Pause and _____ .

Instead of being overwhelmed by an emotion, our detachment allows us to reset and explore our options for moving forward. With the separation in place, we can now do the deeper sensemaking that is needed. In the last phase of the workshop exercise, we practice *thoughtful sensemaking* with a simple but essential "pause-and-reframe" practice that expands our pausing into a more complete response.

While pausing starts the process with a mindful separation from the triggering emotion, there is still work to be done. As soon as we can sense that we are ready to be "open for business," we begin to move to the upward spiral strategies that work best for us and the situation.

• *Reframe the situation*	• *Take action*
• *Accept the situation*	• *Gain understanding*
• *See the positive*	• *Be resilient*
• *Forgive and forget*	• *Problem-solve*
• *Remain open*	• *Get creative*

While negative emotions narrow our focus and can create a downward spiraling of actions (we are closed for business), the positive strategies above do the opposite by broadening our outlook and potential responses (I am open for business).[23] As a result, we are less likely to obsess over a problem and more likely to reframe it in a more positive way.[24] Said more simply:

The pause-and-reframe response keeps us open for business!

> Here's an example: I am frustrated by a colleague's lack of follow-through on a shared project. I can sense my energy flowing into a downward spiral (*why can't they be more responsible?*), but I catch myself and pause. I reframe the situation in the moment to … *I need to better understand their situation so that we can move forward in a more positive way.*

> Here's another example: A friend sends an unsettling comment but I am deep into completing a special phase of a project that will take at least another hour. I begin to dwell on the comment, and the subsequent negative feelings remind me to pause. In this case I will suppress my feelings until I can deal with them more effectively.

In both examples above, the "pause and reframe" response has given me the best chance for a positive outcome. Plus, I avoided the potential downward spiral that my initial negative emotions were triggering. We have all had that experience of making things worse than they really are.

> *"You're up one day and the next you're down.*
> *It's half an inch of water and you think you're gonna drown."*
> **— John Prine**

Over time we actually get good at this pause-and-reframe response and build a repertoire of potential responses. For me personally, I have improved significantly over time, but that was not always the case. As a young manager, I can now see how easy it was for me to fall into the downward spiral. A missed deadline, no matter how insignificant, would often lead to extreme feelings of "worry" followed by "awfulizing" the things that would happen next. I am not kidding when I reveal that I could easily turn a small mistake at work into the inevitability of being homeless!

It takes time to create the kind of behavioral flexibility needed to navigate the emotional challenges of a chaotic world. But the new personal resources that will accrue, such as resilience and mindfulness, will facilitate one's personal growth and sense of purpose in life. Little by little, positive emotions (although fleeting) can expand our mindsets in ways that will reshape who we will become.

Here's an additional insight that I still carry with me today.

How a person experiences their day can be best understood by their positivity ratio (which is the ratio of their positive to negative emotions).[25] Since negative emotions tend to carry more influence than positive ones, it follows that positive emotions need to outnumber them. Research has identified a 3-to-1 ratio (positive to negative) as the needed tipping point for us to see our lives as positive overall and with the potential to flourish. We don't need to actually track positive-vs-negative emotions as they occur. Intuitively we will know when we are out of balance. More importantly, we protect against this imbalance with our pause-and-reframe practice, which will keep us out of the basement of life.

In the table below we show the five triggering events mentioned earlier with the realization that either a downward or upward spiral has the potential to occur. Again, we have a choice. The first triggering example (the data in the report doesn't make sense) leads to an emotional reaction of CONFUSION. This confusion could lead us to disregard the report or possibly lay blame on its source. It's not hard to imagine how things could continue to get worse, spiraling down. The pause-and-reframe responses, developed by workshop participants, start with reframing the "confusing data" as a challenge to better understand. Participants also created illustrative responses for the other triggering events. The key is not to feel pressure to fully resolve the problem but to …

… get it out of the emotional danger zone with an initial and positive framing.

Here's the reality. Not every challenge will be successfully concluded. We get that. But we can leverage the pause-and-reframe response to give us our best chance. In the heat of the moment (when emotions are at play), we learn to pause and choose a positive framing as shown in the five examples below. This pause-and-reframe ritual keeps us out of a downward spiral that can totally derail our days.

Triggering Event	Negative Emotions	Pause and Reframe
The data in the report doesn't make sense.	CONFUSED	*Reframe as a challenge. Be curious and start to explore options.*
A sick child interrupts our intended schedule for the day.	ANXIOUS	*Accept the situation and reframe as an opportunity to show compassion and spend time with a loved one.*
A colleague fails to deliver promised information ... again.	ANGRY	*Give the benefit of the doubt by gaining more understanding as to why and be ready to move on.*
A small mistake I just made could have a significant impact on others.	FEARFUL	*Be totally transparent and determine how "impacted others" would like you to respond.*
We fret on how to best recover from an overreaction with a family member.	GUILT	*Apologize (no matter who is at fault) and let the air out so things don't get worse.*

Review and Reflect

Our practice of thoughtful sensemaking gives us our best chance to keep our days on track despite the inevitable disruptions. The cool thing is that, over time, this practice also develops an incredible capacity to complement our insanely human speed of thought (and its misuses) with the uniquely human pacing of thoughtfulness. While sensemaking is natural, it is our capacity for thoughtful sensemaking that is the differentiator in *everydayness*.

While emotions can be disruptive, thoughtful sensemaking acknowledges their vital role in creating the necessary pause points in our over-packed days. As we saw with sadness, our emotions can slow us down, connect us to others, and facilitate the kind of meaningful moments that feel uniquely human.

In sum, sensemaking is a way of being as we pause, rethink, reconcile, and give enough space to the feelings that define our days. We're not throwing out the rational mind. We seek to empower it through a deeper, wiser self. When successful, a more humble, compassionate, and loving person emerges.

I end with the notion that there is no ultimate meaning in life. It is made up of a myriad of smaller meanings that we create and connect together in the moments of every day. I leave you with one of my favorite quotes:

> *"The only Zen you find on tops of mountains is the Zen you bring there."*
> — **Robert M. Pirsig**

Chapter Five
Mindsets, Routines, and Rituals

Don't forget the secret sauce

"We are what we repeatedly do."
— Aristotle

Key Themes	Questions We Will Answer
Mindsets Matter	*What are the mindsets we are cultivating through everydayness?*
Routines Are Good	*What important role do routines play in our days?*
Rituals Are Special	*Why are rituals essential to everydayness?*

Mindsets Matter

We started with a lesson from the pandemic, revealing how our capacity for meaning-making can prevail under the most difficult circumstances. In our journey together we also explored how three core sources of meaning (appreciation, purpose, and sensemaking), could serve as the essential practices for reclaiming our days in a chaotic, post-pandemic world. While our contemporary lives can leave us feeling disconnected, fragmented, and without purpose, *everydayness* provides a new roadmap for reclaiming and living our days more fully.

In the frameworks below we reveal how each of the three practices is supported by an empowering mindset that is brought to life with daily routines and rituals. A mindset is a set of beliefs that shape how we make sense of the world and ourselves. They influence how we think, feel, and behave in our daily interactions. In short, they have the potential to greatly impact *what we do* and *who we are* in the most positive ways. The opposite is also true. Without a supporting mindset, new routines and behaviors will lose their sense of purpose over time. In other words, it is hard to be *generous* without a mindset of *generosity*.

In our first practice of *appreciation*, we focused on building a mindset of *time abundance*. Knowing that we have 20,000 waking moments every day, we shift our thinking from "I don't have enough time" to "I have plenty of time to do what matters most." We do this through "minding the moments" with the notion that it just takes one moment to make a difference in someone's life. With the Greek time frames of *Chronos* and *Kairos*, we also create a language that helps us move from living on clock time (which we don't have enough of) to expanding time by slowing to a *Kairos* "in-the-moment" pacing.

Essential to this mindset of appreciation is the "pause." When we pause between activities, we open ourselves up to discovering a new kind of presence. When we rush from one thing to another, we gloss over the surface of life, losing our connection to not just the important things but to the humanness found in the most ordinary of moments. Summarized below is our appreciation mindset.

Practice	Mindset
Appreciation	From: Not enough time To: Plenty of time to do what matters most. We do so by pausing to bring a special presence to our daily experiences.

In our second practice of *purpose*, we bring the loftiness of the "what is your purpose in life" question down to ground level, acknowledging that our special calling or purpose may evolve over time and through new experiences. A new question helps to facilitate the emergent nature of finding our true north: *What would you be doing every day in your most meaningful life?*

Practice	Mindset
Purpose	Each day has a purposeful beginning that is facilitated by our carefully crafted intentions, allowing us to grow our sense of purpose and ourselves.

Our third practice, *sensemaking,* gives us our best chance to keep our days on track despite the inevitable disruptions and barriers. While emotions can be disruptive, *thoughtful* sensemaking acknowledges (paradoxically!) their vital role in creating the necessary pause points in our fragmented days. Thoughtfulness not only influences how we do our work but who we want to become.

Practice	Mindset
Sensemaking	"Being thoughtful" slows us to a meaning-making pace that allows us to proactively manage our feelings and the unexpected challenges that triggered them.

With these mindsets serving as the necessary foundation, we are now ready to explore how our routines and rituals bring them to life.

Routines Are Good

How we feel on one day will be different from how we feel on other days. Sometimes significantly! A day can start off well but in a matter of seconds we can go from thriving to barely surviving as the chaos, uncertainty, and complexity of life prevails. It could be one of those mini-crises on the home front or some bad news in our work environment. Maybe we're just feeling down from the long work hours. Or it could be that nagging virus we just can't seem to shake.

Surely most of us have found that having daily routines can bring at least some stability and order to this chaos and uncertainty. That's because routine and structure can give us a sense of control and predictability, helping us to feel safe and secure. In our personal lives, even having meals around the same time can give us something to anchor our time to. Of course, much of our day at work can revolve around well-established routines (e.g., the Monday morning staff meeting). How we actually do our work often follows a specific routine. Even surgeons and pilots will follow a checklist to free them up from having to remember all of the details, allowing them to do their best work.

Consider this scenario. As you are boarding your plane for a fourteen-hour flight, you look to the left in the cockpit where the pilots sit. Surely you are hoping their routine from the previous night granted them a deep and restful sleep and their morning routine that got them to the airport was ... well ... *routine*. In fact, you would probably hope that just about everything in their life epitomized stability. You certainly don't want them trying anything new in their piloting routines. Our wish for them is simple:

Fly the plane. Fly the plane. Fly the plane.

Of course, when an emergency does strike, solid routines can save the day. Famously, airline pilot Captain "Sully" Sullenberger became a source of inspiration after his successful emergency water landing of a disabled airliner on the Hudson River. As Sully noted, what made it possible was following a well-established routine. So routines can also have dramatic impacts beyond just doing the same old thing over and over again.

One of my favorite sports examples is from tennis star Rafa Nadal. The Spaniard has dominated the French Open over the years and is considered one of the best ever. He is also known for his wide range of quirky routines (from pre-serve rituals to jumping during the coin toss to how he drinks his water and energy drink during changeovers). These routines, and many others, are done over and over, whether he wins or loses. But because they are done routinely, it creates a stable environment where he can focus on excelling.

The reality is that most of us, like Rafa, are seeking to build the kinds of routines that will support the "less-scripted" or creative parts of our lives. When I am authoring a book, I rely on my routines to create the necessary space to write for significant periods of time. A first grade school teacher may rely heavily on routines to create the necessary stability in the classroom. A CEO, no matter how big their staff, is not relieved of the pressure to create the kinds of routines in both their work and personal lives that give them the necessary freedom to truly lead. The automatic nature of our routines requires little psychic energy, reserving our personal resources for the more complex, creative, or unplanned challenges of the day.

My own personal experience is that routines not only provide stability and a sense of control but they can also bring comfort. My morning routine is simple and officially starts with a great cup of coffee. After savoring a few sips, I will do my first e-mail review of the day (mostly to get it out of the way). I resist checking the news until later (bad news can wait). I now turn to my first ritual of the day: setting my daily intentions, both above the line and below the line. I love this simple process of crafting the day with the things that matter most (as well as some non-negotiable priorities like getting my taxes submitted on time). This morning routine typically allows for some reading before starting my first scheduled activity or meeting. While certainly not reflecting the discipline of a Navy Seal, I find my "comfortable" morning routine a perfect start for me. While it only lasts about thirty minutes or so, it is a rhythm that centers me for my intention setting while protecting me (at least temporarily) from the human messiness that will inevitably make its way into the day.

Finally, by bringing more routine into our lives, we have the potential to actually save time and free it up for the more essential things in our days. A great example is how we manage e-mail. Most of us are jumping in and out of our devices all day, wreaking havoc on our capacity to be attentive to the task at hand. A new routine might build around "scheduled review times," forgoing the ongoing disruption and creating actual response time (instead of re-visiting the same e-mails over and over). Since most routines are process-driven, my simple prescription is to develop a step-by-step process that works for you. (By the way, there are tons of great books and supporting resources on habits, routines, systems, etc.). Over time, these process-driven behaviors become automatic, releasing us to do more important things. We have now reached a critical pause point in our discussion:

Routines are good. Rituals are special.

Rituals Are Special

While the repetition and automatic nature of our routines can bring stability to our chaotic days, it is rituals that create the magic we long for. A routine is typically a consistent, step-by-step process. A hydration routine could be drinking eight glasses of water during the day. A ritual, on the other hand, slows to a more mindful and meaningful pace. It could be the true enjoyment of that first cup of tea in the morning or the evening walk that helps to put the day (and our minds) to rest.

While routines create the structure of the dance floor,
rituals allow us to dance.

Rituals appear regularly in our holiday events and ceremonies of all kinds (e.g., graduations, retirements, promotions, etc.). What characterizes a ritual is the richness and symbolism of the elements that make it up. I will argue that they represent the secret sauce for bringing *everydayness* to life. It is why I saved this section of the book until last. Think of rituals as meaning-making routines that are brought to life by a special "I am here" presence. A ritual creates the special energy we feel at a celebration (and wish we had more access to in routine situations).

Here's a simple example. While a parent may have a solid routine that gets their child ready for bed, it is the bedtime-story ritual that creates special moments for both and prepares the child to enter the dark night feeling safe and secure. In other words, rituals bring a special connection to how we experience time, ourselves, and those we are linked to in this world. While routines bring stability to our days, rituals facilitate meaning-making. While routines are built around process steps, rituals are non-linear in nature and create a different kind of presence. It is important to remember:

Rituals are always done in Kairos time.

We expand our sense of time when we drop into a *Kairos* presence. This is because the pressure of clock time fades as we become present to the moment, which will feel increasingly expansive. Think of that special lunch with your best friend where you lose yourself to the joyous, spontaneous, and unfolding experience. Now imagine the difference between a parent who treats story time as just one more step in the bedtime routine versus a parent who can make that shift into *Kairos* time, where they can get lost in the moment. The same goes for just about all of our activities as we decide what time frame we will *purposely* move into.

If you think about it, *everydayness,* by its nature, is best built around rituals. In fact, our three practice areas each feature a core ritual that brings it to life.

Practice	Ritual
Appreciation	Minding the moments by *Savoring*
Purpose	Cultivating a sense of purpose through *Intention setting*
Sensemaking	Promoting thoughtful sensemaking with a *Pause-and-reframe* response

These three rituals, covered in depth in their respective chapters, are just a start—*a great start.* Ultimately, we want to continue adding rituals to not only expand our sense of time but our impact. Granted, our days will benefit from routines and time management, but only to the degree that they free us up to develop new rituals.

Below are examples of three more rituals that have made a difference to workshop participants. You probably do or have done these things in the past. The key will be to convert them more fully to the special status of a ritual. Let's briefly review each of these keepers!

Practice	Ritual
Appreciation	Gratitude
Purpose	Goal-setting
Sensemaking	Conversation

Gratitude: This expression of gratitude may feel like one of those optional "feel good" steps. Actually, it is much more. This step has the potential to transform both us and the quality of our days. While we tend to think of gratitude as a feeling, research continues to demonstrate its value as an ongoing ritual as we learn to appreciate what surrounds us.[26] It starts with a simple appreciation for the goodness in life—our family, friends, and the little dog sitting on our lap. We then learn to let it follow us throughout the day. Increasingly we catch ourselves pausing to appreciate the little blessings that could easily go unnoticed. It is something we learn to do throughout the day, counting our blessings as we go. When we do so, all kinds of benefits accrue, starting with our physical and mental health and extending to our relationships, resilience, and self-esteem.[27]

Goal-setting: What brings our intention setting to life at the beginning of the day is the ongoing development of overarching "life" goals that set our overall direction for personal growth and development. It is these "big" goals that illuminate the larger course from which we navigate our days. Beyond the traditional work goals and objectives, I find few people who routinely develop and refine their "life" goals. When they committed to writing their goals down and treated this as a ritual, a whole new world opened up.

Meaningful conversation: Conversation is central to our lives, but in many respects it has lost its relevance, as technology is the increasingly preferred medium that connects us. An e-mail, text, or post simply can't replace the meaning-making capabilities of a conversation. In fact, it is through conversation that we enhance our sensemaking, shape our possibilities, and form the relationships that we so need and desire.

Part of the challenge is that we simply don't like to slow to the speed of conversation. It takes more time, more psychic energy, and more skill than an e-mail or text. Too often our conversations feel one-way, transactional, and overly efficient. We need to return conversation to "ritual status"—dropping into *Kairos* time to create a special flow of meaning between participants.

> *"The notion that our lives succeed or fail on conversations one at a time is at once commonsensical and revolutionary."*
> **— Ken Blanchard**

Let's keep going. How about translating some of our *work routines* into rituals to infuse them with a new spirit? I picked three obvious ones that are favorites with workshop participants to get the wheels turning. In the framework below I will start the discussion by posing a question.

Work Rituals	Description
Meetings	Why not bring some ritual "magic" to the dreaded (and often soul-sucking) meeting routine that has become *too routine*? How about adding a "fun" topic to the agenda? It doesn't have to be time-consuming to create a spark.
Work Processes	What parts of our work processes could benefit from more presence and intentionality? One idea is to pick one important part of the process where you intentionally pause and drop into *Kairos* time.
Communications	How can we bring some new energy to our communication routines (written or otherwise) that over time turn dull? Try telling a story to humanize the points you need to make or add a photo that relates to your audience. (A great "pic" always opens us up.)

Just about every domain of our lives can benefit from a bit of "ritualization" (where we bring a more meaningful sense of attention to the experience). Here are three more related to our well-being. Let's explore.

Well-being Rituals	Description
Exercise	Let's face it, exercise can be a drab experience. Why not replace some time spent on a machine with a hike that brings you in touch with nature?
Sleep	Increasingly, we are seeing huge connections between well-being and sleep. Why not create a pre-sleep ritual (e.g., favorite reading material) to facilitate the nod-off with grace and ease?
Reading	We continue to read less and less and spend more and more time in front of screens. How about a reading ritual with the family that protects forty minutes a day to shift that balance?

You get the idea. Over time we can become "ritual rich" in our days. None of the potential rituals noted above are new to us. Many, like meetings and exercise, are existing routines that could benefit from some new "ritual energy." Routines are actions that just need to be done, and rituals require a more appreciative, purposeful, or sensemaking mindset where true meaning can occur.

Review and Reflect

Everydayness is greatly enabled and energized through routines and rituals. They feel like two sides of the same coin, with each playing a necessary role in living our days to the fullest. The structure of routine provides the stability that allows us the freedom to guide our rituals as needed. For example, managing e-mail with a more efficient routine may free us up to be more creative (and more ritual-like) in our other communications.

I want to add one more "nudge" to our approach. As we move between routines and rituals, there is always a *transition space* that represents an important pause point that will keep us true to our *everydayness* practices. For example, as I return home from work, I am moving from my work life to home life. I symbolically use my front door as a transition point to acknowledge:

I am home now.

Touching the doorjamb as I enter, I am intentionally creating some separation from "work Mike" as I become more fully present to my at-home rituals. My cat Gus, who always greets me at the door, is my furry reminder to make the transition. One mom in our workshops, Elise, says she has learned to not enter her home, with two little girls eagerly waiting, until she is ready to be Mom. As Elise shared:

> *"Excited to be home, my body would rush in, but my head was still at work with some issue. That never worked well as my girls were now demanding my full attention. Now I will walk around the block until I am truly ready to be Mom."*

In *everydayness*, these thoughtful transitions occur not only between physical spaces but any time we transition. A great example is when we are shifting between *Chronos* time (I am efficiently processing my e-mails) to *Kairos* time (where a single e-mail will require a uniquely creative response). Just this simple recognition allows us to take a deep breath and feel ourselves moving from a "just do it" mindset to a more thoughtful presence.

I am here. There is no other place I would rather be.

Final Thoughts for the Journey Forward

The Velvet Underground was an American rock band that originated in New York City in 1964. The front man for the band was legendary rocker Lou Reed. The oft-repeated story is that, although their first album sold only a few thousand copies, everyone who bought the album started a band. I have a similar aspiration for this book. I'm not sure how many books will be sold, but I am hoping that everyone who buys it will start their own unique "brand" of *everydayness*. To that end, here are seven key takeaways that will hopefully bring *everydayness* to life for you:

One: Act like you have plenty of time. Actually, we really do … with 20,000 new moments rolling into our personal accounts every day, we have plenty of time to do what matters most. So, mind the moments in ways that bring meaning to you and those around you. Remember, it takes just one moment to make someone's day.

Two: Slow to a savoring pace. To savor is to fully experience the coffee, the conversation, the cat on our lap. We move from "consuming" to "fully experiencing" the precious moments of our days. (Guess what? They are all precious because they are all we have.)

Three: Do things on purpose. Do things that matter most. Get out of the busyness trap. Learn to say no to the meaningless stuff that can consume too much of our lives. Keep cultivating a sense of purpose, even if some larger, more profound purpose in life remains elusive. Remember, most of the meaning we find is in the day-to-day journey itself. I try to remember Mother Teresa's sentiment that none of us can do great things, but we can do small things with great love.

Four: Be intentional. Be super intentional. Begin the day spending the necessary *Kairos* time to define the intentions that will go "above the line." Don't forget to tap into your powerful, 24/7 personal assistant (the RAS), which will bring you new ideas, introduce you to people, and keep you focused on the things that matter most.

Five: Be thoughtful. Thoughtfulness, when present, gives us the feeling that we are not just reacting but responding fully to a person or situation. It feels great when we can slow to this "human-centered" pacing. More than anything, it is what people want most from us. So let's give it to them.

Six: Be positive. The pause-and-reframe response is essential to countering the inevitable negative emotions that can leave us in "survival mode." Proactively, we reframe the negative emotions we are experiencing, giving us our best chance for initiating positive emotions (which can become the dominant force in our days).

Seven: Move from "routines" to "rituals." *Everydayness* is built around the special pacing of rituals. It is less about getting things done and more about finding meaning in what we do. Over time, little by little, and where appropriate, we transition routines into meaning-making rituals.

Beyond these seven takeaways, my best advice is to start slowly and purposely by learning to pause. It is from this simple act that all kinds of good things happen. When we pause, even for a moment, we become smarter. We also become …

More emotionally intelligent.
More present.
More purposeful.
More intentional.
More thoughtful.
More positive.

So we pause. When we are confused, we pause. When we transition to something new, we pause. When we are stuck, we pause. Just for the heck of it, we pause.

With our pausing practice well-established, we are now ready to reshape not only *what we do* but *who we are*:

Appreciative, purposeful, and thoughtful souls.

When we consistently pause between activities in our days, a deeper and more authentic presence takes over. It replaces the "I'm so busy" persona, the persona that lives on the surface, missing out on the meaningful moments that when fully experienced …

… tell a story … your story.

I will see you on the path.

Mike

> "Everything is held together with stories. That is all that is holding us together, stories and compassion."
> — **Barry Lopez**

Opportunities to Connect

You can learn more about Michael Morrison, PhD, a trailblazer in leadership development and intentional living by connecting with him on LinkedIn, where he routinely shares new posts and articles to keep the discussion going.

You can also join Mike and other journeyers in a free **Everydayness Community** that features weekly posts and supportive resources on Everydayness topics, chat opportunities to present questions and share ideas, and live webinars. Go to everydayness.com to sign-up for these free services.

Finally, to explore coaching or consulting with Mike, you can contact him directly at mike_morrison@me.com. His one-on-one insight and expertise have provided differentiating value to clients across the globe.

Let's embark on a journey of growth and impactful leadership together!

Thank You

Dear Reader,

Thank you for taking the time to read my book, Everydayness. I genuinely hope you found its content inspiring and impactful.

Would you please take a moment to share your thoughts on Everydayness by leaving a brief review? Your verified review helps not only me as a self-publishing author to reach more people, it also helps others like you discover the insights and value this book offers.

Whether it inspired a new perspective and enhanced your understanding or gave you simple yet effective tools to engage your life with more purpose and meaning, your review is invaluable. I deeply appreciate and welcome all feedback.

Thank you for sharing your thoughts and contributing to the discussion!

Onward,

Mike

About the Author

Mike Morrison, Ph.D., is the founder of the University of Toyota. His consulting and coaching work has taken him around the globe in service to a range of leading enterprises. He is the author of *Leading Through Meaning: A Philosophical Inquiry*, *The Other Side of the Card*, and *Creating Meaningful Change*. He currently resides in Los Angeles with his wife, Kerry, and their two cats, Gus and Angelina. Their adult children, Zack and Mackenzie, live in New York and Los Angeles, respectively.

in www.linkedin.com/in/mike-morrison-ph-d-580b0b14

Notes

1 Michael F. Steger, Shigehiro Oishib, and Todd B. Kashdan, "Meaning in life across the life span: Levels and correlates of meaning in life from emerging adulthood to older adulthood," *The Journal of Positive Psychology*, Vol. 4, No. 1 (January 2009): 43–52.

2 John Gardner, "Personal Renewal" speech delivered to McKinsey & Company, Phoenix, AZ, November 10, 1990.

3 Viktor E. Frankl, *Man's Search for Meaning* (Boston: Beacon Press, 1992), 98–111.

4 Martin Seligman, *Flourish: A Visionary New Understanding of Happiness and Well-being* (Atria Books, 2012), 11–16.

5 Viktor E. Frankl, *Man's Search for Meaning* (Boston: Beacon Press, 1992), 99–111.

6 Michael F. Steger, Shigehiro Oishib, and Todd B. Kashdan, "Meaning in life across the life span: Levels and correlates of meaning in life from emerging adulthood to older adulthood," *The Journal of Positive Psychology*, Vol. 4, No. 1 (January 2009): 43–52. Note: While Steger and other researchers consistently refer to the elements of purpose and sensemaking elements as core sources of meaning, I add "appreciation" as my third source in alignment with the ideas of both classic (Frankl, see footnote 5) and contemporary scholars (Steger, see footnote 1) where "experiential appreciation" is viewed as another unique indicator of meaning in life.

7 Viktor E. Frankl, *Man's Search for Meaning* (Boston: Beacon Press, 1992), 99–111.

8 Viktor E. Frankl, *Man's Search for Meaning* (Boston: Beacon Press, 1992), 99–111.

9 Jinhyung Kim, Patricia Holte, Frank Martela, et al, "Experiential Appreciation as a pathway to meaning in life," *Nature Human Behaviour*, Vol 6 (May 2022): 677–690.

10 Matthew B. Crawford, *The World Beyond Your Head* (NY: Farrar, Straus and Giroux, 2015), 14–17.

11 Shihui Feng, Yip Kan Wong, Lai Yin Wong, Liaquat Hossain, "The Internet and Facebook Usage on Academic Distraction of College Students," *Computers & Education Journal*, Vol 134 (June 2019): 41–49.

12 Matthew B. Crawford, *The World Beyond Your Head* (NY: Farrar, Straus and Giroux, 2015), 14–17.

13 James Hollis, *The Middle Passage* (Toronto: Inner City Books, 2021), 17–27.

14 Vivek H. Murthy, Together: *The Healing Power of Human Connection in a Sometimes Lonely World* (NY: Harper, 2020), 151–184.

15 Daniel Kahneman and Jason Riis, "Living, and Thinking about It: Two Perspectives on Life," in *The Science of Well-Being*, ed. F.A. Huppert, N. Baylis, and B. Keverne (Oxford University Press, 2005), 285–304.

16 James Nestor, *Breath* (NY, Riverhead Books, 2020), 143–145.

17 James Hollis, *The Middle Passage* (Toronto: Inner City Books, 2021), 17–27.

18 Ryan M. Niemiec, Tayyab Rashid, and Marcello Spinella, "Strong Mindfulness: Integrating Mindfulness and Character Strengths," *Journal of Mental Health Counseling* 34, no. 3 (July 2012): 240–253.

19 Michael F. Steger, Shigehiro Oishib, and Todd B. Kashdan, "Meaning in life across the life span: Levels and correlates of meaning in life from emerging adulthood to older adulthood," *The Journal of Positive Psychology*, Vol. 4, No. 1 (January 2009): 43–52.

20 Viktor E. Frankl, *Man's Search for Meaning* (Boston: Beacon Press, 1992), 17–18.

21 James Hollis, *The Middle Passage* (Toronto: Inner City Books, 2021), 40–43.

22   Catherine Travis, "Kind, Considerate, Thoughtful: A Semantic Analysis," *Lexikos* (Series 7: 1997): 130–152.

23   Eric Garland, Barbara Frederickson, Ann M. Kring, et al, "Upward Spirals of Positive Emotions Counter Downward Spirals of Negativity," *Clinical Psychology Review* (November 2010): 849–864.

24   Eric Garland, Barbara Frederickson, Ann M. Kring, et al, "Upward Spirals of Positive Emotions Counter Downward Spirals of Negativity," *Clinical Psychology Review* (November 2010): 849–864.

25   Barbara Fredrickson, M. Losada, "Positive affect and the complex dynamics of human flourishing," *American Psychologist* 60 (7) (2005): 678–686.

26   Annamaria Di Fabio, Letizia Palazzeschi, and Ornella Bucci, "Gratitude in Organizations: A Contribution for Healthy Organizational Contexts," *Frontiers in Psychology Journal* (November 2017): 1-6.

27   Annamaria Di Fabio, Letizia Palazzeschi, Ornella Bucci, *Frontiers in Psychology Journal* (November 2017): 1–6. Note: Also see a summarizing article by Amy Morin, "7 Scientifically Proven Benefits of Gratitude," *Psychology Today*, Posted April 3, 2013 (https://www. psychologytoday.com/gb/blog/what-mentally-strong-people-dont-do/20 1504/7-scientifically-proven-benefits-of-gratitude).

Made in the USA
Middletown, DE
23 October 2024